Ghosts, Spirits, and the Afterlife in Native American Indian Mythology And Folklore

Written and Edited by G.W. Mullins
With Original Art by C.L. Hause

© 2019 by G.W. Mullins and C. L. Hause

All rights reserved. No part of this book may be reproduced, stored in a retrieval system or transmitted in any form or by any means without the prior written permission of the publishers, except by a reviewer who may quote brief passages in a review to be printed in a newspaper, magazine or journal.

ISBN: 978-1-64713-312-2
Second Edition Printing

Light Of The Moon Publishing has allowed this work to remain exactly as the author intended, verbatim, without editorial input.

Printed in the United States of America

The following book represents a collection of Native American works which are public domain. You may have read the stories before. In true story telling fashion, the stories have been left as close to the original form as possible. In Native American culture, in order to pass the stories along with all information intact, they had to be told pretty much word for word, to keep the legends alive. Many of these stories were translated directly from original Native language texts. With that in mind, please be aware that some spellings and word usage may vary from one tribe to another. For instance, the spelling of "teepee", as used in this book, can also be written as "tipi", and "tepee". All are correct. Also, when using words like "someone", in most native cultures, it would be "some one". So, keep in mind, these are not necessarily misspellings. They are simply dialect and translations.

For information about the book and novel releases of
G.W. Mullins please visit his web site at
http://gwmullins.wix.com/officialsite

All images contained in this book are original works by
C.L. Hause. For more information on his art and other projects
please visit his web page at http://clarencehause.wix.com/homepage

Also Available From G.W. Mullins And C.L. Hause

War Song Tales Of The Native American Indians

Walking With Spirits Native American Myths, Legends, And Folklore
Volumes One Thru Six

The Native American Cookbook

Native American Cooking - An Indian Cookbook With Legends And Folklore

The Native American Story Book - Stories Of The American Indians For Children
Volumes One Thru Five

The Best Native American Stories For Children

Cherokee A Collection of American Indian Legends, Stories And Fables

Creation Myths - Tales Of The Native American Indians

Strange Tales Of The Native American Indians

Spirit Quest - Stories Of The Native American Indians

Animal Tales Of The Native American Indians

Medicine Man - Shamanism, Natural Healing, Remedies And Stories Of The Native American Indians

Native American Legends: Stories Of The Hopi Indians
Volumes One and Two

Totem Animals Of The Native Americans

The Best Native American Myths, Legends And Folklore
Volumes One Thru Three

Ghosts, Spirits And The Afterlife In Native American Indian Mythology And Folklore

The Native American Art Book – Art Inspired By Native American Myths And Legends

Star People, Sky Gods And Other Tales Of The Native American Indians

Story Teller – An Anthology Of Folklore From The Native American Indians

Red Road - Legends Of The Native American Indians

Origin Tales Of The Native American Indians

Animal Tales Of The Native American Indians Vol. 2

Sioux Legends Of The Lakota, Dakota, And Nakota Indians

THE NATIVE AMERICAN STORY COLLECTION SERIES

Featuring The Writing Of Best-Selling Author
G.W. MULLINS
And Original Art From Award Winning Artist
C.L. HAUSE

The Native American Story Book Series

Tales Of The Native American Indians Series

Native American Cooking, Art And Medicine Books

Walking With Spirits Native American Myths, Legends, And Folklore Series

The Best Native American Native American Myths, Legends And Folklore

- Walking With Spirits Volumes 1 thru 6 Native American Myths, Legends, And Folklore
- The Native American Cookbook
- Native American Cooking - An Indian Cookbook With Legends And Folklore
- The Native American Story Book Volumes 1 thru 3 Stories Of The American Indians For Children
- Creation Myths - Tales Of The Native American Indians
- Strange Tales Of The Native American Indians
- Animal Tales Of The Native American Indians
- Spirit Quest Native American Indian Legends Stories and Fables
- Medicine Man - Shamanism, Natural Healing, Remedies And Stories Of The Native American Indians
- Cherokee A Collection of American Indian Legends, Stories And Fables
- Native American Legends: Stories Of The Hopi Indians Volumes One and Two
- The Native American Art Book
- The Best Native American Native American Myths, Legends And Folklore

LIGHT OF THE MOON PUBLISHING

This book includes historical materials that may imply negative stereotypes reflecting the culture or language of a particular period or place. These items are presented as part of the historical record and should not be interpreted to mean that the author in any way endorses the stereotypes implied.

This book is dedicated to Vince Mullins, my Grandfather (Pawpaw). A tall red man who I loved so much. I think he would have liked this.
G.W. Mullins

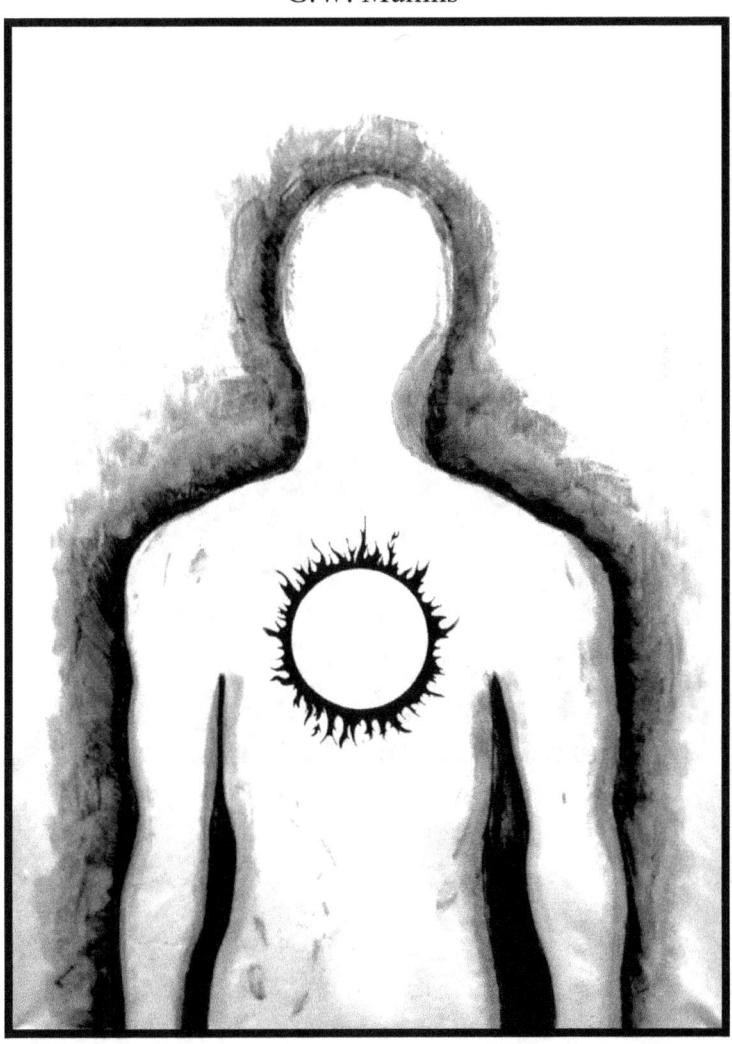

"May the stars carry your sadness away,
May the flowers fill your heart with beauty,
May hope forever wipe away your tears,
And, above all, may silence make you strong."

...Chief Dan George (1899-1981)

Chief Dan George, (July 24, 1899 – September 23, 1981) was a chief of the Tsleil-Waututh Nation, a Coast Salish band located on Burrard Inlet in North Vancouver, British Columbia, Canada. He was also an author, poet, actor, and an Officer of the Order of Canada. At the age of 71, he was nominated for an Academy Award for Best Supporting Actor in Little Big Man.

A Speech to the Dead by Native American (Luiseno) Chief Fox:

"Now this day you have ceased to see daylight.
Think only of what is good.
Do not think of anything uselessly.
You must think all the time of what is good.
You will go and live with our nephew.
And do not think evil towards these your relatives.
When you start to leave them this day you must not think backwards of them with regret.
And do not think of looking back at them.
And do not feel badly because you have lost sight of this daylight.
This does not happen today to you alone, so that you thus be alone when you die.
Bless the people so that they may not be sick.
This is what you will do.
You must merely bless them so that they may live as mortals here.
You must always think kindly.
Today is the last time I shall speak to you.
Now I shall cease speaking to you, my relative."

Table of Contents

A Speech to the Dead 10
Introduction 11
Ghost of the White Deer 14
The Story of a Poor Man 16
The Resuscitation of the only Daughter 18
The Spirit Bride 23
Heavy Collar and the Ghost Woman 25
Bluejay finds a Wife 34
Two Ghostly Lovers 37
Origin of the Medicine Man 42
The Medicine Grizzly Bear 46
A Little Brave and the Medicine Woman 64
The Man Who Was Afraid of Nothing 67
The Ghosts' Buffalo 73
The Land of the Dead 76
Blue Jay Visits Ghost Town 79
The Spirit Land 86
The Skin Shifting Old Woman 87
The Spirit Wife 94
The Nunne'hi and Other Spirit Folk 101
The Spirit Defenders of Nikwasi' 110
The Haunted Whirlpool 113
Deer Hunter and White Corn Woman 115
A Journey to the Skeleton House 119
The Elk Spirit Of Lost Lake 125
The Fatal Swing 128
The Simpleton's Wisdom 131
The Ghost Country 135
The Legend of the Maid of the Mist 137
Ghost Stallion 139
Song of the Ghost Dance 142
The Deserted Children 143
How the Worm Pipe Came to the Blackfoot 149
Tale of Coyote and the Origin of Death 152

Introduction

A few words about Native Americans, Ghosts and Spirits:

Native American history is filled with stories about animals, creation of the Earth and man, life lessons and of course ghosts...

Ghosts, spirits, and the "walking dead" were often known to pay visits to their family and those left behind. Many of these stories revolved around lost loves and attempts to reclaim the person taken from them. Other stories spun tales of revenge and payback for those who wronged them. In any case death was looked at as a doorway to the afterlife and not to be feared.

The Native American belief in spirit and ghost visitation can be found in a speech made in 1854, by Chief Seattle:

"And when the last red man shall have perished from the earth and his memory among white men shall have become a myth, these shores shall swarm with the invisible dead of my tribe, and when your children's children shall think themselves alone in the field, the store, the shop, upon the highway or in the silence of the woods, they will not be alone. ... the dead are not powerless. Dead - I say? There is no death. Only a change of worlds."" - Chief Seattle, 1854

While many cultures passed their history through the written word, most Native American tribes had no written language. The Cherokees were one of the leaders in recording their lifestyles and tradition. As in true tribal fashion most information was passed through stories and in song to the beat of a drum. Many of these stories are included within the pages of this book.

You will be given many opportunities to relive the past cultures of many tribes and their beliefs in ghosts, spirits and the afterlife. You will be presented with stories of individuals who transcended the plane of death to interact with the living and other spirits who have remained earthbound and troubled who have to work through a life lesson to successfully move on. As is traditional, these stories are here for you to share and pass on to the next generation.

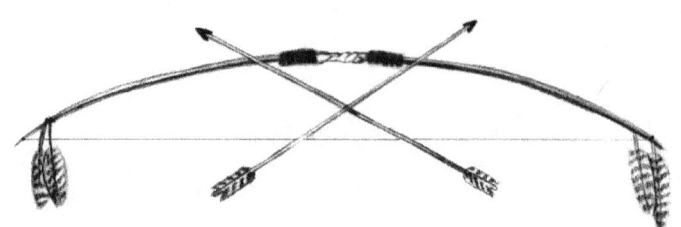

Ghost of the White Deer
Chickasaw
A lore of the Chickasaw People of Oklahoma

A brave, young warrior for the Chickasaw Nation fell in love with the daughter of a chief. The chief did not like the young man, who was called Blue Jay. So the chief invented a price for the bride that he was sure that Blue Jay could not pay.

"Bring me the hide of the White Deer." said the chief. The Chickasaws believed that animals that were all white were magical. "The price for my daughter is one white deer." Then the chief laughed. The chief knew that an 'all white' deer, an albino, was very rare and would be very hard to find. White deerskin was the best material to use in a wedding dress, and the best white deer skin came from the albino deer.

Blue Jay went to his beloved, whose name was Bright Moon. "I will return with your bride price in one moon, and we will be married. This I promise you." Taking his best bow and his sharpest arrows Blue Jay began to hunt.

Three weeks went by, and Blue Jay was often hungry, lonely, and scratched by briars. Then, one night during a full moon, Blue Jay saw a white deer that seemed to drift through the moonlight. When the deer was very close to where Blue Jay hid, he shot his sharpest arrow. The arrow sank deep into the deer's heart. But instead of sinking to his knees to die, the deer began to run. And instead of running away, the deer began to run toward Blue Jay, his red eyes glowing, his horns sharp and menacing.

A month passed and Blue Jay did not return as he had promised Bright Moon. As the months dragged by, the tribe decided that he would never return.

But Bright Moon never took any other young man as a husband, for she had a secret. When the moon was shining as brightly as her name, Bright Moon would often see the white deer in the smoke of the campfire, running, with an arrow in his heart. She lived hoping the deer would finally fall, and Blue Jay would return.

To this day the white deer is sacred to the Chickasaw People, and the white deerskin is still the favorite material for the wedding dress.

The Story of a Poor Man

Adapted from Alanson Skinner, The Mascoutens or Prairie Potawatomi Indians, Part III, Mythology and Folklore, Milwaukee Public Museum Bulletin

Once there was a poor orphan who was not well brought up. He was respected by no one and never got invited to feasts or ceremonies. Despite this, he managed to get married and went hunting by himself on foot or with his canoe. He usually had very little luck hunting, but once he killed a deer. He built a little shelter to stay overnight, started to cook the deer meat, and sat down to rest with his dog beside him. He smoked and dozed, and after a while he opened his eyes and saw a person standing there.

He looked again and the person vanished. He thought it was strange that his dog had not seemed to notice that anyone was there. The man turned his meat on the fire and, looking up again, saw two men there. They seemed poor and unable to speak. The man greeted them and said, "My friends, you frightened me. I am poor. No one brought me up to know what to do under these circumstances. I would like to know who you are, but I do not know how to ask." The two smiled and nodded to him in a friendly manner, so he went on: "Well, I shall feed you, and do what I can for your comfort." They nodded again. "Are you ghosts?" the hunter asked. Again they smiled and bowed, so he began to broil meat on the coals, as one does for the souls of the dead.

The man was camped right in the middle of an ancient and forgotten cemetery and since the ghosts were there, he thought that might be the case. He offered prayers to the dead and prayed for the safety of his wife and child. He promised to make a feast for these people who were long dead and forgotten and promised to always mention the names of the two visitors, or at least to speak of them.

The next day he killed four bucks and luck went with him wherever he traveled. When he got home, he told his wife what had happened, and how he had been frightened when the two speechless men stood there. He told her to help him prepare a feast for them, although he did not know their names. He hoped that these ghosts would help them to become accepted by society. He invited one of the honorable men of the tribe, and told him of his strange adventure. He explained that he did not know how to go about giving a feast of the dead, and he turned it over to the elder man. The old man said that the poor man had done the right thing, and that the appearance of these ghosts was a good omen. So the feast was held.

A long time passed, and the poor man became a very great hunter, but he never forgot to sacrifice holy tobacco to the two spirits. After a long while, he became one of the leaders of the tribe, and remained faithful to the memory of the two ghosts he had met.

The Resuscitation of the only Daughter
Sioux

There once lived an old couple who had an only daughter. She was a beautiful girl, and was very much courted by the young men of the tribe, but she said that she preferred single life, and to all their heart-touching tales of deep affection for her she always had one answer. That was "No."

One day this maiden fell ill and day after day grew worse. All the best medicine men were called in, but their medicines were of no avail, and in two weeks from the day that she was taken ill she lay a corpse. Of course there was great mourning in the camp. They took her body several miles from camp and rolled it in fine robes and blankets, then they laid her on a scaffold which they had erected. (This was the custom of burial among the Indians). They placed four forked posts into the ground and then lashed strong poles lengthwise and across the ends and made a bed of willows and stout ash brush. This scaffold was from five to seven feet from the ground. After the funeral the parents gave away all of their horses, fine robes and blankets and all of the belongings of the dead girl. Then they cut their hair off close to their heads, and attired themselves in the poorest apparel they could secure.

When a year had passed the friends and relatives of the old couple tried in vain to have them set aside their mourning. "You have mourned long enough," they would say. "Put aside your mourning and try and enjoy a few more pleasures of this life while you live. You are both growing old and can't live very many more years, so make the best of your time." The old couple would listen to their advice and then shake their heads and answer: "We have nothing to live for. Nothing we could join in would be any amusement to us, since we have lost the light of our lives."

So the old couple continued their mourning for their lost idol. Two years had passed since the death of the beautiful girl, when one evening a hunter and his wife passed by the scaffold which held the dead girl. They were on their return trip and were heavily loaded down with game, and therefore could not travel very fast. About half a mile from the scaffold a clear spring burst forth from the side of a bank, and from this trickled a small stream of water, moistening the roots of the vegetation bordering its banks, and causing a growth of sweet green grass. At this spring the hunter camped and tethering his horses, at once set about helping his wife to erect the small tepee which they carried for convenience in traveling.

When it became quite dark, the hunter's dogs set up a great barking and growling. "Look out and see what the dogs are barking at," said the hunter to his wife. She looked out through the door and then drew back saying: "There is the figure of a woman advancing from the direction of the girl's scaffold."

"I expect it is the dead girl; let her come, and don't act as if you were afraid," said the hunter. Soon they heard footsteps advancing and the steps ceased at the door. Looking down at the lower part of the door the hunter noticed a pair of small moccasins, and knowing that it was the visitor, said: "Whoever you are, come in and have something to eat."

At this invitation the figure came slowly in and sat down by the door with head covered and with a fine robe drawn tightly over the face. The woman dished up a fine supper and placing it before the visitor, said: "Eat, my friend, you must be hungry." The figure never moved, nor would it uncover to eat. "Let us turn our back towards the door and our visitor may eat the food," said the hunter. So his wife turned her back towards the visitor and made herself very busy cleaning the small pieces of meat that were hanging to the back sinews of the deer which had been killed. (This the Indians use as thread.) The hunter, filling his pipe, turned away and smoked in silence. Finally the dish was pushed back to the woman, who took it and after washing it, put it away. The figure still sat at the door, not a sound coming from it, neither was it breathing. The hunter at last said: "Are you the girl that was placed upon that scaffold two years ago?" It bowed its head two or three times in assent. "Are you going to sleep here tonight; if you are, my wife will make down a bed for you." The figure shook its head.

"Are you going to come again tomorrow night to us?" It nodded assent.

For three nights in succession the figure visited the hunter's camp. The third night the hunter noticed that the figure was breathing. He saw one of the hands protruding from the robe. The skin was perfectly black and was stuck fast to the bones of the hand. On seeing this the hunter arose and going over to his medicine sack which hung on a pole, took down the sack and, opening it, took out some roots and mixing them with skunk oil and vermillion, said to the figure:

"If you will let us rub your face and hands with this medicine it will put new life into the skin and you will assume your complexion again and it will put flesh on you." The figure assented and the hunter rubbed the medicine on her hands and face. Then she arose and walked back to the scaffold. The next day the hunter moved camp towards the home village. That night he camped within a few miles of the village. When night came, the dogs, as usual, set up a great barking, and looking out, the wife saw the girl approaching.

When the girl had entered and sat down, the hunter noticed that the girl did not keep her robe so closely together over her face. When the wife gave her something to eat, the girl reached out and took the dish, thus exposing her hands, which they at once noticed were again natural. After she had finished her meal, the hunter said: "Did my medicine help you?" She nodded assent. "Do you want my medicine rubbed all over your body?" Again she nodded. "I will mix enough to rub your entire body, and I will go outside and let my wife rub it on for you." He mixed a good supply and going out left his wife to rub the girl. When his wife had completed the task she called to her husband to come in, and when he came in he sat down and said to the girl: "Tomorrow we will reach the village. Do you want to go with us?" She shook her head. "Will you come again to our camp tomorrow night after we have camped in the village?" She nodded her head in assent. "Then do you want to see your parents?" She nodded again, and arose and disappeared into the darkness.

Early the next morning the hunter broke camp and traveled far into the afternoon, when he arrived at the village. He instructed his wife to go at once and inform the old couple of what had happened. The wife did so and at sunset the old couple came to the hunter's tepee. They were invited to enter and a fine supper was served them. Soon after they had finished their supper the dogs of the camp set up a great barking. "Now she is coming, so be brave and you will soon see your lost daughter," said the hunter. Hardly had he finished speaking when she entered the tent as natural as ever she was in life. Her parents clung to her and smothered her with kisses.

They wanted her to return home with them, but she would stay with the hunter who had brought her back to life, and she married him, becoming his second wife. A short time after taking the girl for his wife, the hunter joined a war party and never returned, as he was killed on the battlefield.

A year after her husband's death she married again. This husband was also killed by a band of enemies whom the warriors were pursuing for stealing some of their horses. The third husband also met a similar fate to the first. He was killed on the field of battle.

She was still a handsome woman at the time of the third husband's death, but never again married, as the men feared her, saying she was holy, and that any one who married her would be sure to be killed by the enemy.

So she took to doctoring the sick and gained the reputation of being the most skilled doctor in the nation. She lived to a ripe old age and when she felt death approaching she had them take her to where she had rested once before, and crawling to the top of the newly erected scaffold, wrapped her blankets and robes about her, covered her face carefully, and fell into that sleep from which there is no more awakening.

The Spirit Bride

An Algonquin Legend

There was once a young warrior whose bride died on the eve of their wedding. Although he had distinguished himself by his bravery and goodness, the death left the young man inconsolable.

He was unable to eat or sleep. Instead of hunting with the others, he just spent time at the grave of his bride, staring into the air.

However, one day he happened to overhear some elders speaking about the path to the spirit world. He listened intently and memorized the directions to the most minute detail. He had heard that the spirit world was far to the south. He immediately set out on his journey. After two weeks, he still saw no change in the landscape to indicate that the spirit world was near.

Then he emerged from the forest and saw the most beautiful plain he had ever seen. In the distance was a small hut where an ancient wise man lived. He asked the wise man for directions.

The old man knew exactly who the warrior was and whom he sought. He told the lad that the bride had passed by only a day before. In order to follow her, the warrior would have to leave his body behind and press on in his spirit. The spirit world itself is an island in a large lake that can be reached only by canoes waiting on this shore. However, the old man warned him not to speak to his bride until they were both safely on the island of the spirits.

Soon the old man recited some magic chants and the warrior felt his spirit leave his body. Now a spirit, he walked along the shore and saw a birch bark canoe. Not a stone's throw away was his bride, entering her own canoe. As he made his way across the water and looked at her, he saw that she duplicated his every stroke. Why didn't they travel together? One can only enter the spirit world alone and be judged only on one's individual merits.

Midway through the journey, a tempest arose. It was more terrible than any he had ever seen. Some of the spirits in canoes were swept away by the storm-these were those who had been evil in life. Since both the warrior and his bride were good, they made it through the tempest without incident and soon the water was as smooth as glass beneath a cloudless sky.

The island of the blessed was a beautiful place where it was always late spring, with blooming flowers and cloudless skies, never too warm or too cold. He met his bride on the shore and took her hand. They had not walked ten steps together when a soft sweet voice spoke to them-it was the Master of Life.

The Master told them that the young warrior must return as he came; it wasn't his time yet. He was to carefully trace his steps back to his body, put it on, and return home. He did this and became a great chief, happy in the assurance that he would see his bride once again.

Heavy Collar and the Ghost Woman

A Blackfoot Legend

The Blood camp was on Old Man's River, where Fort McLeod now stands. A party of seven men started to war toward the Cypress Hills. Heavy Collar was the leader. They went around the Cypress Mountains, but found no enemies and started back toward their camp. On their homeward way, Heavy Collar used to take the lead. He would go out far ahead on the high hills, and look over the country, acting as scout for the party. At length they came to the south branch of the Saskatchewan River, above Seven Persons' Creek. In those days there were many war parties about, and this party traveled concealed as much as possible in the coulees and low places.

As they were following up the river, they saw at a distance three old bulls lying down close to a cut bank. Heavy Collar left his party, and went out to kill one of these bulls, and when he had come close to them, he shot one and killed it right there. He cut it up, and, as he was hungry, he went down into a ravine below him, to roast a piece of meat; for he had left his party a long way behind, and night was now coming on. As he was roasting the meat, he thought, for he was very tired, "It is a pity I did not bring one of my young men with me. He could go up on that hill and get some hair from that bull's head, and I could wipe out my gun." While he sat there thinking this, and talking to himself, a bunch of this hair came over him through the air, and fell on the ground right in front of him. When this happened, it frightened him a little; for he thought that perhaps some of his enemies were close by, and had thrown the bunch of hair at him. After a little while, he took the hair, and cleaned his gun and loaded it, and then sat and watched for a time. He was uneasy, and at length decided that he would go on further up the river, to see what he could discover. He went on, up the stream, until he came to the mouth of the St. Mary's River. It was now very late in the night, and he was very tired, so he crept into a large bunch of rye-grass to hide and sleep for the night.

The summer before this, the Blackfeet (Sik-si-kau) had been camped on this bottom, and a woman had been killed in this same patch of rye-grass where Heavy Collar had lain down to rest. He did not know this, but still he seemed to be troubled that night. He could not sleep. He could always hear something, but what it was he could not make out. He tried to go to sleep, but as soon as he dozed off he kept thinking he heard something in the distance. He spent the night there, and in the morning when it became light, there he saw right beside him the skeleton of the woman who had been killed the summer before.

That morning he went on, following up the stream to Belly River. All day long as he was traveling, he kept thinking about his having slept by this woman's bones. It troubled him. He could not forget it. At the same time he was very tired, because he had walked so far and had slept so little. As night came on, he crossed over to an island, and determined to camp for the night. At the upper end of the island was a large tree that had drifted down and lodged, and in a fork of this tree he built his fire, and got in a crotch of one of the forks, and sat with his back to the fire, warming himself, but all the time he was thinking about the woman he had slept beside the night before. As he sat there, all at once he heard over beyond the tree, on the other side of the fire, a sound as if something were being dragged toward him along the ground. It sounded as if a piece of a lodge were being dragged over the grass. It came closer and closer.

Heavy Collar was scared. He was afraid to turn his head and look back to see what it was that was coming. He heard the noise come up to the tree in which his fire was built, and then it stopped, and all at once he heard some one whistling a tune. He turned around and looked toward the sound, and there, sitting on the other fork of the tree, right opposite to him, was the pile of bones by which he had slept, only now all together in the shape of a skeleton. This ghost had on it a lodge covering. The string, which is tied to the pole, was fastened about the ghost's neck; the wings of the lodge stood out on either side of its head, and behind it the lodge could be seen, stretched out and fading away into the darkness. The ghost sat on the old dead limb and whistled its tune, and as it whistled, it swung its legs in time to the tune.

When Heavy Collar saw this, his heart almost melted away. At length he mustered up courage, and said: "Oh ghost, go away, and do not trouble me. I am very tired; I want to rest." The ghost paid no attention to him, but kept on whistling, swinging its legs in time to the tune. Four times he prayed to her, saying: "Oh ghost, take pity on me! Go away and leave me alone. I am tired; I want to rest." The more he prayed, the more the ghost whistled and seemed pleased, swinging her legs, and turning her head from side to side, sometimes looking down at him, and sometimes up at the stars, and all the time whistling.

When he saw that she took no notice of what he said, Heavy Collar got angry at heart, and said, "Well, ghost, you do not listen to my prayers, and I shall have to shoot you to drive you away." With that he seized his gun, and throwing it to his shoulder, shot right at the ghost. When he shot at her, she fell over backward into the darkness, screaming out: "Oh Heavy Collar, you have shot me, you have killed me! You dog, Heavy Collar! There is no place on this earth where you can go that I will not find you; no place where you can hide that I will not come."

As she fell back and said this, Heavy Collar sprang to his feet, and ran away as fast as he could. She called after him: "I have been killed once, and now you are trying to kill me again. Oh Heavy Collar!" As he ran away, he could still hear her angry words following him, until at last they died away in the distance. He ran all night long, and whenever he stopped to breathe and listen, he seemed to hear in the distance the echoes of her voice. All he could hear was, "Oh Heavy Collar!" and then he would rush away again. He ran until he was all tired out, and by this time it was daylight. He was now quite a long way below Fort McLeod. He was very sleepy, but dared not lie down, for he remembered that the ghost had said that she would follow him. He kept walking on for some time, and then sat down to rest, and at once fell asleep.

Before he had left his party, Heavy Collar had said to his young men: "Now remember, if any one of us should get separated from the party, let him always travel to the Belly River Buttes. There will be our meeting-place." When their leader did not return to them, the party started across the country and went toward the Belly River Buttes. Heavy

Collar had followed the river up, and had gone a long distance out of his way; and when he awoke from his sleep he too started straight for the Belly River Buttes, as he had said he would.

When his party reached the Buttes, one of them went up on top of the hill to watch. After a time, as he looked down the river, he saw two persons coming, and as they came nearer, he saw that one of them was Heavy Collar, and by his side was a woman. The watcher called up the rest of the party, and said to them: "Here comes our chief. He has had luck. He is bringing a woman with him. If he brings her into camp, we will take her away from him." And they all laughed. They supposed that he had captured her. They went down to the camp, and sat about the fire, looking at the two people coming, and laughing among themselves at the idea of their chief bringing in a woman. When the two persons had come close, they could see that Heavy Collar was walking fast, and the woman would walk by his side a little way, trying to keep up, and then would fall behind, and then trot along to catch up to him again. Just before the pair reached camp there was a deep ravine that they had to cross. They went down into this side by side, and then Heavy Collar came up out of it alone, and came on into the camp.

When he got there, all the young men began to laugh at him and to call out, "Heavy Collar, where is your woman?" He looked at them for a moment, and then said: "Why, I have no woman. I do not understand what you are talking about." One of them said: "Oh, he has hidden her in that ravine. He was afraid to bring her into camp." Another said, "Where did you capture her, and what tribe does she belong to?" Heavy Collar looked from one to another, and said: "I think you are all crazy. I have taken no woman. What do you mean?" The young man said: "Why, that woman that you had with you just now: where did you get her, and where did you leave her? Is she down in the coulee? We all saw her, and it is no use to deny that she was with you. Come now, where is she?" When they said this, Heavy Collar's heart grew very heavy, for he knew that it must have been the ghost woman; and he told them the story. Some of the young men could not believe this, and they ran down to the ravine, where they had last seen the woman. There they saw in the soft dirt the tracks made by Heavy Collar, when he went down into the ravine, but there were no other tracks near his, where they had seen the woman walking. When they found that it was a ghost that had come along with Heavy Collar, they resolved to go back to their main camp. The party had been out so long that their moccasins were all worn out, and some of them were footsore, so that they could not travel fast, but at last they came to the cut banks, and there found their camp seven lodges.

That night, after they had reached camp, they were inviting each other to feasts. It was getting pretty late in the night, and the moon was shining brightly, when one of the Bloods called out for Heavy Collar to come and eat with him. Heavy Collar shouted, "Yes, I will be there pretty soon." He got up and went out of the lodge, and went a little way from it, and sat down. While he was sitting there, a big bear walked out of the brush close to him. Heavy Collar felt around him for a stone to throw at the bear, so as to scare it away, for he thought it had not seen him. As he was feeling about, his hand came upon a piece of bone, and he threw this over at the bear, and hit it. Then the bear spoke, and said: "Well, well, well, Heavy Collar; you have killed me once, and now here you are hitting me. Where is there a place in this world where you can hide from me? I will find you, I don't care where you may go." When Heavy Collar heard this, he knew it was the ghost woman, and he jumped up and ran toward his lodge, calling out, "Run, run, a ghost bear is upon us!"

All the people in the camp ran to his lodge, so that it was crowded full of people. There was a big fire in the lodge, and the wind was blowing hard from the west. Men, women, and children were huddled together in the lodge, and were very much afraid of the ghost. They could hear her walking toward the lodge, grumbling, and saying: "I will kill all these dogs. Not one of them shall get away."

The sounds kept coming closer and closer, until they were right at the lodge door. Then she said, "I will smoke you to death." And as she said this, she moved the poles, so that the wings of the lodge turned toward the west, and the wind could blow in freely through the smoke hole. All this time she was threatening terrible things against them. The lodge began to get full of smoke, and the children were crying, and all were in great distress almost suffocating. So they said, "Let us lift one man up here inside, and let him try to fix the ears, so that the lodge will get clear of smoke." They raised a man up, and he was standing on the shoulders of the others, and, blinded and half strangled by the smoke, was trying to turn the wings. While he was doing this, the ghost suddenly hit the lodge a blow, and said, "Un!" and this scared the people who were holding the man, and they jumped and let him go, and he fell down. Then the people were in despair, and said, "It is no use; she is resolved to smoke us to death." All the time the smoke was getting thicker in the lodge.

Heavy Collar said: "Is it possible that she can destroy us? Is there no one here who has some strong dream power that can overcome this ghost?"

His mother said: "I will try to do something. I am older than any of you, and I will see what I can do." So she got down her medicine bundle and painted herself, and got out a pipe and filled it and lighted it, and stuck the stem out through the lodge door, and sat there and began to pray to the ghost woman. She said: "Oh ghost, take pity on us, and go away. We have never wronged you, but you are troubling us and frightening our children. Accept what I offer you, and leave us alone."

A voice came from behind the lodge and said: "No, no, no; you dogs, I will not listen to you. Every one of you must die."

The old woman repeated her prayer: "Ghost, take pity on us. Accept this smoke and go away."

Then the ghost said: "How can you expect me to smoke, when I am way back here? Bring that pipe out here. I have no long bill to reach round the lodge." So the old woman went out of the lodge door, and reached out the stem of the pipe as far as she could reach around toward the back of the lodge. The ghost said: "No, I do not wish to go around there to where you have that pipe. If you want me to smoke it, you must bring it here." The old woman went around the lodge toward her, and the ghost woman began to back away, and said, "No, I do not smoke that kind of a pipe." And when the ghost started away, the old woman followed her, and she could not help herself.

She called out, "Oh my children, the ghost is carrying me off!" Heavy Collar rushed out, and called to the others, "Come, and help me take my mother from the ghost." He grasped his mother about the waist and held her, and another man took him by the waist, and another him, until they were all strung out, one behind the other, and all following the old woman, who was following the ghost woman, who was walking away.

All at once the old woman let go of the pipe, and fell over dead. The ghost disappeared, and they were troubled no more by the ghost woman.

Bluejay finds a Wife

A Chinook Legend

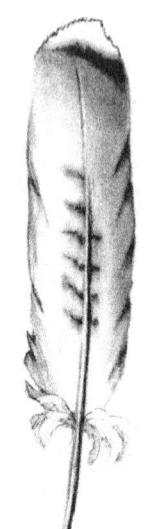

Bluejay was a trickster who enjoyed playing clever tricks on everyone, especially his sister Ioi. As she was the eldest sister, Blue Jay was supposed to obey her.

But he deliberately misinterpreted what she said, excusing himself by saying, "Ioi always tells lies."

Ioi decided that it was high time for Bluejay to quit his playful life of trickery and settle down with a wife. She told him that he must select a wife from the people of the land of the dead, who were called the "Supernatural People." Ioi recommended that Blue Jay choose an old woman for a wife and suggested the recently deceased wife of a chief.

But Bluejay balked; he wanted a young and attractive woman. He found the corpse of a beautiful young girl and took it to Ioi, who advised him to take the body to the land of the dead to be revived.

Bluejay set out on this journey and arrived at the first village of the Supernatural People.

They asked him, "How long has she been dead?"

"Only a day," he answered.

The Supernatural People of the first village then informed him that there was nothing they could do to help him; he must go on to the village where people who were dead for exactly one day were revived.

Bluejay arrived at the second village the next day and asked the people to revive his wife. The people here too asked him how long she had been dead.

"Two days now," he replied. "There is nothing we can do; we only revive those who were dead exactly one day." So Bluejay went on.

He reached the third village on the day after that and asked the people to revive this wife.

"How long has she been dead?" they asked.

"Exactly three days now."

"Most unfortunate," they replied. "We can only revive those who have been dead exactly two days."

And so it went on from village to village until Bluejay finally came to the fifth village, where the people could at last help him. The people of the fifth village liked Bluejay and made him a chief. But the trickster tired of the Underworld and wanted to take his newly revived wife back to the land of the living.

When Bluejay arrived at home with his wife, her brother saw she was alive once more and ran to tell their father, an old chief, who demanded that Blue Jay cut off all of his hair as a gift to his new in-laws.

When there was no response from Bluejay, the chief became angry and led a party of male relatives to find him. Just as they nearly caught him, Bluejay assumed the form of a bird and flew off again to the land of the dead.

At this, his wife's body fell to the ground, lifeless. She went to meet her husband in the land where he was now an exile.

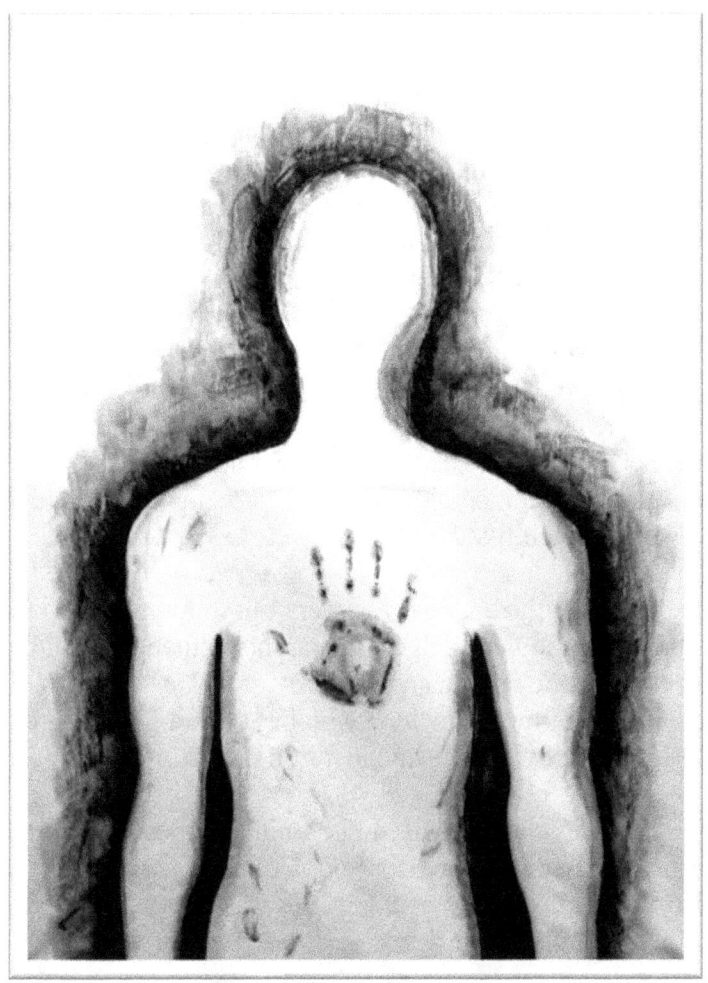

Two Ghostly Lovers
Brule, Sioux
*--Told by Lame Deer at Winner Rosebud Indian Reservation, South Dakota, 1970.
Recorded by Richard Erdoes*

Long ago there lived a young, good-looking man whom no woman could resist. He was an elk charmer--a man who had elk medicine, which carries love power. When this man played the *siyotanka*, the flute, it produced a magic sound. At night a girl hearing it would just get up and go to him, forsaking her father and mother, her own lover, or husband. Maybe her mind told her to stay, but her heart was already beating faster and her feet were running.

Yet the young man, the elk charmer himself, was a lover with a stone heart. He wanted only to conquer women, the way a warrior conquers an enemy. After they came to him once, he had no more use for them. So in spite of his wonderful powers, he did not act as a young man should and was not well liked.

One day when the elk charmer went out to hunt buffalo, he did not return to the village. His parents waited for him day after day, but he never came back. At last they went to a special kind of medicine man who has "finding stones" that give him the power to locate lost things and lost people.

After this holy man had used his finding stones, he told the parents: "I have sad news for you. Your son is dead, and not from sickness or an accident. He was killed. He is lying out there on the prairie."

The medicine man described the spot where they would find the body, it was as he had said. Out on the prairie their son was lying dead, stabbed through the heart. Whether he had been killed by an enemy warrior or a wronged husband from his own tribe, or even a discarded, thrown-away girl, no one ever knew.

His parents dressed him in his finest war shirt, which he had loved more than all his women, and in dead man's moccasins, whose soles are beaded with spirit-land designs. They put his body up on the funeral scaffold, and then the tribe left that part of the country. For it was a very bad thing, this killing which was probably within the tribe. It was, in fact, the very worst thing that could happen, even though everybody was thinking that the young man had brought it on himself.

One evening many days' ride away, when the people had already forgotten this sad happening and were feasting in their tipis, all the dogs in camp started howling. Then the coyotes in the hills took up their mournful cry. Nobody could discover the reason for all this yowling and yipping. But when it finally stopped, the people could hear the hooting of many owls, speaking of death and ghostly things. The laughter in the camp stopped. The fires were put out, and the entry flaps to the tipis were closed.

People tried to sleep, but instead they found themselves listening. They knew a spirit was coming. Finally they heard the unearthly sounds of a ghost flute and a voice they knew very well--the voice of the dead young man with the elk medicine. They heard this voice singing:

Weeping I roam.
I thought I was the only one
Who had known many loves,
Many girls, many women,
Too many of them.
Now I am having a hard time.
I am roaming, roaming,
And I have to keep roaming
As long as the world stands.

After that night, the people heard the song many times. A lone girl coming home late from a dance, a young woman up before sunrise to get water from the stream, would hear the ghostly song mixed with the sound of the flute. And they would see the shape of a man wrapped in a gray blanket hovering above the ground, for even as a ghost this young man would not leave the girls alone.

Well, it happened long ago, but even now the old-timers at Rosebud, Pine Ridge, and Cheyenne River are still singing this ghost song.

Now, there was another young man who also had a cold heart. He too made love to too many girls and soon threw them away. He was a brave warrior though. He was out a few times with a girl who was in love with him, and he said he would marry her. But he didn't really mean it; he was like many other men who make the same promise only to get under a girl's blanket. One day he said: "I have to go away on a horse stealing raid, I'll be back soon, and then I'll marry you." She told him: "I'll wait for you forever!"

The young warrior went off and never came back; he forgot all about her. The girl, however, waited for a long time.

Well, this young man roamed about for years and had many loves. Then one time when he was hunting, he saw a fine tipi. It had a sun-and-moon design painted on it. He recognized it immediately: it was the tipi of the girl he had left long ago. "Is she still good-looking and loving?" he wondered. "I'll find out!"

He went inside, and there was the girl, lovelier than ever. She was dressed in a white, richly quilled buckskin dress. She smiled at him. "My lover, have you come back at last?" After serving him a fine meal, she helped him take off his moccasins and his war shirt. She traced his scars from many fights with her fingers. "My warrior," she said, "lie down here beside me, on this soft, soft buffalo robe." He lay down and made love to her, and it was sweeter than he had ever experienced, sweeter than he could have imagined. Then she said: "Rest and sleep now."

The young man--though not very young anymore--woke up in the morning and saw the morning sun shining into the tipi. But the tipi was no longer bright and new; it was ragged and rotting. The buffalo robe under which they had slept was almost hairless and full of holes. He lifted the robe and pulled it aside to look at the girl, and instead of a living, beautiful woman, he found a skeleton. A few strands of black hair still adhered to the skull, which seemed to smile at him. They young girl had died there long ago, waiting for him to come back. He had made love to a spirit. He had embraced bones. He had kissed a skull. He had coupled with a skeleton!

As the thought sank in, the warrior cried aloud, jumped up, and began running in great fear running he knew not where. When he finally came to, he was *witko*, mad. He spoke in strange sounds. His eyes wandered. His thoughts went astray. He was never right in his mind again.

Origin of the Medicine Man
A Passamaquoddy Story

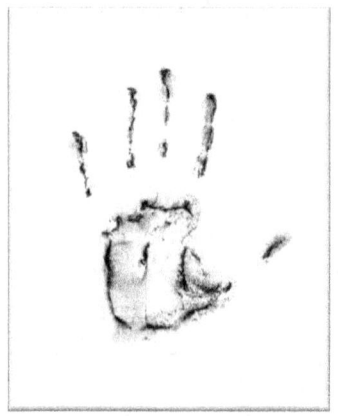

The Medicine Man is Glooscap, the Good-Spirit. Legend has it that the father of Glooscap is a being who lives under a great waterfall beneath the earth. His face is half-red, and he has a single all- seeing eye. He can give to anyone coming to him the medicine he desires. Glooscap is still busy sharpening his arrows off in a distant place, preparing sometime to return to earth and make war.

Passamaquoddies tell all of their old stories as truth. But of other stories, they speak of them as "what they hear," or hearsay.

This is a legend of long, long ago about a Passamaquoddy Indian woman who travelled constantly back and forth and through the woods. From every bush she came to, she bit off a twig, and from one of these she became pregnant. Bigger and bigger she grew, until at last she could not travel, but she built a wigwam near the mouth of a fresh-running stream.

In the night, the woman gave birth to a child. She thought at first that she should kill the child. Finally, she decided to make a bark canoe in which she placed her child. She set it adrift and let it float down the stream. Though the water was rough in places, the child was not harmed, or even wet.

The canoe floated to an Indian village, where it became stranded on the sandy shore near a group of wigwams. One of the women found the baby and brought it to her home. Every morning thereafter, it seemed that a baby of the village died. The villagers did not know what was the matter with their babies.

A neighbor noticed how the rescued child toddled off to the river every night and returned shortly after. She wondered if this could have anything to do with the death of so many babies. Then she saw the child return to its wigwam with a small tongue, roast it, and eat it. Then it lay down to sleep all night.

On the next morning, a report circulated that another child had died. Then the Indian woman was certain she knew who the killer was. She alerted the parents of the dead child and found that the child's tongue had been removed, and the child had bled to death.

Tribal deliberations were held to decide what should be done with the murderer. Some said, cut up the person and throw him into the river. Others said, burn the fragments; this they did after much consultation. They burned the fragments of the wayward child, until nothing but its ashes remained.

Naturally, everyone understood the child was dead. But that night it came back to camp again with a small tongue, which it roasted and ate. The next morning another child was found to have died in the night. The weird child was found sleeping in its usual place, just as before its cremation. He said to everyone that he would never kill any more children and that now he had become a big boy, in fact.

The big boy announced he would take one of his bones out of his side. This he started to do, and all of his bones spilled out of his body at the same time. He closed his eyes by drawing his fingers over his eyelids, hiding his eyes. He could not move without bones and he began to grow very fat.

He surprised the Passamaquoddies by becoming a great Medicine Man. Anything they desired within reason, he granted. Later, however, his tribe moved away from their old camp. Before they left, they built a fine wigwam for the Medicine Man. So accustomed had they become to call upon his powers that they still returned to make their requests. His tribal members asked him for medicine of all kinds. When he granted their wishes, he asked them, "Turn me over and you will find your medicine beneath me."

A young man came and wished to have the love of a woman, so he asked for a love potion. The Medicine Man said, "Turn me over." The young man turned over the conjurer and found an herb. "You must not give this away or throw it away," said the old man. The young Passamaquoddy went back to his own wigwam.

Soon he was aware that all the young women followed him in the camp, at all times. In fact, he longed to be alone for a change. He did not like to be chased by the women. At last when he became too troubled by the tribal women, he returned to the Medicine Man and gave back the herbal love portion. The young Passamaquoddy left without it.

Another young man went to the conjurer for help. The Medicine Man asked, "What is it you want?" This man said, "I want to live as long as the world shall stand."

"Your request is a hard one to consider, but I will do my best to answer it," replied the Medicine Man. "Now turn me over," and underneath his body was an herb. He said, "Go to a place that is bare of everything, so bare it is destitute of all vegetation, and just stand there." The Medicine Man pointed out this direction for the young man.

The young man went according to the Medicine Man's instructions, but looking back at the conjurer, the standing man saw branches and twigs sprouting all over his own body. He had been changed into a cedar tree, to stand there forever--useless to everyone.

The Medicine Grizzly Bear

*A Pawnee Legend
George Bird Grinnell,
Published in
Harper's monthly
magazine, 1901*

A long time ago there lived in a camp of Pawnees a certain poor boy. His father had only one pony. Once he had been a leading man in the tribe, but now he seemed to be unlucky.

When he went on the war-path he brought back nothing, and when he fought he did nothing, and the people did not now look up to him.

There was a chief's son who loved the poor boy, and these two went together all the time. They were like brothers; they used to hunt together and go courting together, and when they were traveling, the poor boy often rode one of the ponies of the chief's son, and the latter used to go to the poor boy's lodge and sleep there with him.

Once the camp went off to hunt buffalo, and the poor boy and the chief's son rode together all the time. After the people had made camp at a certain place, the chiefs decided to stop here for four days, because the buffalo were close by, and they could kill plenty and dry the meat here. North of the camp was a hill on which grew many cedar-trees, and during the day the poor boy had overheard people saying that many Indians had been killed on that hill, among those trees. They said that no one ought to go there, for it was a dangerous place.

That night the chief's son went over to his friend's lodge to sleep there, but before they went to bed he left the lodge for a time, and while he was gone the poor boy, as he sat there waiting, began to think about himself and how unhappy he was. He remembered how poor he and his father were, and how everybody looked down on them and despised them, and it did not seem to him that things would ever be any better for them than they were now. For a long time he sat there thinking about all these things, and the more he thought of them the worse they seemed, and at last he felt that he was no longer glad to live, and he made up his mind to go up into those cedars.

He went out of the lodge and started to go up toward the trees. It was bright moonlight, so that he could see well. Just before he reached the edge of the timber he crossed a ravine, and saw there many skeletons of people who had been killed. The ground was white with these bones. He went on into the cedars, and came to a ravine leading up the hills, and followed it. As he went on he saw before him a trail and followed it, and when he came to the head of the ravine there was a big hole in the bank, and the trail led to it. He stopped for a moment when he came to his hole, but then he went in, and when he had entered he saw there, sitting by the fire, a big she-bear and some little cubs.

As the boy stood there looking at her, the she-bear said to him: "I am sorry that you have come here. My husband is the one who kills persons and brings them here for the children and me to eat. You had better go back to your people quickly, or he will eat you up. He has gone hunting, but he will soon be back again. If he finds you here, he will kill you."

The poor boy said: "Well, I came here on purpose to be killed, and I give myself up to you. I shall be glad to be eaten by you. I am here ready to be killed. I am yours. Take me."

The she-bear said: "Oh, I wish I could do something to save you, but I cannot. He is one of those bad bears -- a grizzly -- medicine. I can do nothing for you, but I will try. As soon as you hear any noise outside -- any one coming -- pick up that cub, the littlest one, and hold it in your arms. When he comes in he will tell you to put it down, but do not do so. Hold it tight; he loves that one best of all."

All at once the boy heard outside the cave the noise of a bear snorting and grunting. The she-bear said, "Pick up the cub, quick; he is coming." The boy caught up the little bear, and held it tight to his breast. All at once the noise came to the mouth of the den and stopped. It was the Bear. The boy could hear him talking. He said: "Here! somebody has been about my house. I smell human beings. Yes, he even came in. Where is he? Let me see him, so that I may jump upon him and kill him."

When he came in he saw the boy, and seemed very angry. He stood up on his hind feet and threw up his hands, and then came down again and struck his paws on the ground, and then rose up and snorted "whoof," and blew out red dust from his nostrils, and then came down and jumped about, and sometimes sprang toward the boy, as though he were going to seize him. He was very terrible, and the boy was very much afraid.

The Bear called out to the boy in a loud voice: "How dare

you take up my child and hold it? Let it go, or I will tear you to pieces and eat you." But the boy still held the cub. No matter what the Bear said or what he did, the boy held fast to the cub.

When the Bear saw that the boy would not let the cub go, he became quiet, and no longer seemed angry. He said: "Boy, you are my son. Put down your brother, for now he is your brother. He shall go with you, he shall be your companion, and shall be with you always as your guide and helper. He has told me your story, and how you are poor, unhappy, and now he has kept you from being eaten up. I have taken pity on you, and we will send you back to your people, where you may do some good among them. My son, I am at the head of all these animal lodges, down at Pahuk and at Pahur and everywhere else. I am at the head; there is no animal living that is stronger than I; none that I cannot kill. If a man shoots at me, I make the arrow to fall from my skin without hurting me. Look up around my lodge. See these arrows, these guns, these leggings, these beads, and the medicine that men have brought, thinking to kill me; but I have killed them, and have taken these things, and keep them here."

"I knew that your people were coming to this place to hunt. I drove the buffalo over, so that the people should stop here and hunt and kill meat, in order that you might come to my lodge. I know all your feelings. I know that you are sorry for your poor father, my brother, and I wished you to come here, so that I might make you my son and give my power to you, so that you may become a great man among your people. I know that they are now killing buffalo, and that they will be camped here for four days."

"Now, my son, set your brother free. All the power that I

have I give to you. I shall kill my son, your little brother there, and give you his skin to keep and to carry away with you, so that he may be your companion and may be with you always. Your brother, your friend at the camp, is looking for you, mourning for you, for he thinks you dead, but tomorrow night you shall see him, and shall tell him to rejoice for you and not to mourn. You shall tell him where you have been."

The little bear that he was holding said to the boy: "It is all right now, brother; put me down. My father means what he says. I am glad that I am going to be with you, my brother." The boy put him down.

Then the Bear said to his wife: "Get up. Take that gun." The she-bear took the gun, and they walked around the fireplace in a circle, and sang, and the boy looked on. The Bear took the gun and told the boy to look at them, and to watch carefully everything that they did. After a little he stopped, and shot his wife, and she fell down dead. Then he put down the gun, and went to the she-bear and put his mouth on the wound, and breathed on it and snorted "woof," and sucked in his breath and took the bullet out, and went around the lodge, singing and making motions, and then he took hold of the she-bear and lifted her to her feet, and supported her, and pushed her around, and helped her, and at last she walked, and was well. Then he called the boy to him and said, "Now I will do the same thing to you." And he did the same thing to the boy, and brought him to life in the same way. Then he said, "That is one power I give you to-night."

Then he gave the gun to the boy and went to the other side of the lodge, and sat up, and said, "Now I will open my mouth, and you shoot me right in the mouth." He opened his mouth, and the boy shot him, and he fell over. After a moment he got up on his feet and slapped his paws on his chest several times, and the bullet came out of his mouth, and he walked around the fireplace two or three times, and made motions and grunted, and then he was well. Then he took the boy in his arms, and hugged him and kissed him and breathed on him, and said: "Now I give you my power. Go over there and I will shoot you as you shot me. Do just as I did." The boy went over there, and the Bear shot him, and the boy did just as the Bear had done, and made himself well.

The Bear then put an arrow in the gun and shot it at the boy, and when the smoke cleared away the boy found the arrow fast in his throat, the feather end sticking out. The Bear took it out and made him well, and gave him also this power.

Then the Bear told him to load the gun with a ball and to shoot it at him, and he did so, and shot the Bear, but the lead was made flat and dropped to the ground. The bullet did not go into the Bear.

The Bear now told the boy to take the bow and arrow and to shoot at him with all his strength. The boy did this, but the arrow did not go through the Bear, but the spike rolled up and the shaft was split. The Bear said: "Now you see, my son, that the gun and the bow, the bullet and the arrow, cannot harm me. You shall have the same power. When you go into battle you shall not carry a gun nor arrows, for they are not mine, but you shall take this paint and put it all over your body, then put this feather on your head, and take this club, which is part of my jawbone. All these things have my power and medicine. When you are carrying these things your enemy cannot hurt you, even if you run right on to him; but with one stroke of this club you shall kill your enemy.

The next morning the Bear took the boy out on the prairie and showed him the different roots and leaves of medicines, and told him how to use them; how he should eat some medicine and then he could cure the wounded by just breathing on the wound.

That night the Bear said to him: "Hereafter you shall have the same feelings as the bear. When you get angry, you will have a grunt like a bear; and if you get too fierce, teeth like a bear's will stick out of your mouth, so that the people will know that you are very angry. You shall have my power, and you can go into any of the lodges of the animals, of which I am the chief." And he told him how to get into these lodges.

That day they stayed in the Bear's lodge, and the Bear took the claw off from his little finger and gave it and a little bundle of medicine to the boy. He said, "Take this claw and this bundle of medicine and put them on a string and wear them on your neck always, the claw hanging in front." He taught him how to make plums grow on trees, and how to make ground-cherries come out of his mouth.

That night he sent the boy back to the camp. He said: "Tell your father and mother not to mourn for you, for you will return in two days more. I have driven plenty of buffalo to this place, and they will kill them and dry the meat. Now go to the camp and get a pipe and some tobacco, and bring them here."

The boy went back to the camp. When he went into the lodge his father and mother were glad to see him. He told them not to be anxious about him, and not to say anything about his having been away. Then he went out and found his brother, the chief's son, asleep. He said to him: "Wake up, brother. I want you to get some tobacco and a pipe from your father. Tell no one that it is for me. Bring it here. I want to smoke with you. I am going away again, but you must stay in camp. I will be back in a few days." The chief's son got the things and gave them to the boy. He wanted to go with him, but the poor boy would not let him.

That same night the boy went back to the Bear's den, carrying with him the pipe and tobacco. After he went into the lodge he filled his pipe and lighted it, and he and the Bear smoked together. The Bear said to him: "After you have gone home, whenever you smoke, always point your pipe toward my den and ask me to smoke with you. After lighting your pipe, point it first to Atius Tirawat, and then blow a few whiffs to me. Then I shall know that you still remember me. All my power comes from Atius. He made me. There will be an end to my days as there is to those of every mortal. So long as I live I shall protect you; when I die of old age, you shall die too."

After this he said, "Now bring my youngest boy here." The boy brought the little cub, and the Bear said, "Now kill him." The boy hesitated to do this. He did not want to kill the little bear, but it said to him: "Go on, my brother, kill me. After this I am going to be a spirit, and always to be with you." Then the boy killed him, and skinned him, and tanned his hide. After it was tanned he put some red medicine paint on the hide. When this was done the Bear told him to put his paint, his feathers, and his war-club in this hide, and to wrap them up and make a bundle of them.

Then he said: "Now, my son, go to your people, and when you get home hang your bundle up at the back of the lodge, and let the people know nothing of all this. Keep it secret. Wherever you go, or wherever you are, I shall be with you."

The boy went home to the camp, and told his mother to hang up his bundle, as the Bear had said. Next morning he was in camp and all the people saw him. They were surprised, for they had thought that he had been killed. By this time the Pawnees had all the buffalo they wanted, and the next day they started back to their village.

After they had reached their home, the boy told the chief's son that he wanted him to go off with him on the war-path. His brother said: "It is good. I will go." The poor boy took his bundle, and they started. After traveling many days they came to a camp of the enemy. They went into the village in the daytime, and took many horses and started away with them, riding hard. Soon the enemy pursued them, and at length they could see them coming, and it seemed as if they must soon overtake them. Then the poor boy got off his horse and stopped, telling his brother to go on, driving the horses.

The boy had painted himself red over his whole body. He held his war-club in his hand, and had his feather tied on his head and the little bear-skin on his back. The enemy soon came up and tried to kill him, but they could not. He would run after one and kill him, and all the others would shoot at him with their arrows, but they could not hurt him, and at last they left him and went back, and he went on and overtook the chief's son. Then his brother saw that he had great power.

After this they traveled on slowly, and at last reached the village. His brother told the people that this man was powerful, that they had taken the horses in broad daylight, and the young man had stayed behind on foot and fought the enemy off, while he drove on the horses.

A few days after they reached home a war-party of the

enemy attacked the village. All the Pawnees went out to fight them, but the poor boy stayed behind in the lodge. He took down his bundle, filled the pipe, and pointed it first to Atius, and then toward the Bear's lodge, and smoked. Then he took the paint and mixed it with grease, and rubbed it all over his body except his face: that he painted black.

Then he put the feather on his head and the little bear-robe on his back, and took his war-club in his hand and started out. The Bear had told him that in going into battle he must never start toward the east, but must attack going toward the west. So he went around, and came on the battle-field from one side.

As he came up he saw that his people were having a hard time, and were being driven back. There was one of the enemy who seemed to be the bravest of all. The poor boy rushed at this man and killed him with his club, and then ran back to his own line. When his people looked at him, and saw that it was really the poor boy who had just done so brave a deed, they knew that what the chief's son had said was true. When he started again to rush toward the enemy's line, all the Pawnees followed him.

He ran among the enemy, and with his club killed one here and one there, and the enemy became afraid and ran, and the Pawnees followed and killed many of them. That night they returned to the village, rejoicing over the victory. Everybody was praising the young man. Old men were calling his name, young women were singing about him, and old women dancing before him. People no longer made fun of his father or mother, or of him. Now they looked upon him as a great and powerful person.

The Bear had told him that when he wanted his name changed he must call himself Ku ruks la war uks ti,

Medicine Bear.

That night the Bear came to the boy in his sleep and spoke to him. He said: "My son, tomorrow the chief of the tribe is going to ask you to take his daughter for your wife, but you must not do this yet. I wish you to wait until you have done certain things. If you take a wife before that time, your power will go from you."

The next day the chief came to Medicine Bear and asked him to marry his daughter, and told him the people wanted him to be their head chief. He refused.

Some time after this all the different tribes that had been attacked by him joined forces and came down together to fight the Pawnees. All the people went out to meet them, but he stayed in his lodge and painted himself, and put his feather in his head and the bear-claw on his neck and his bear-skin on his back, and smoked as he always did, and took his club and went out. When he came to the battle, the Pawnees were having a hard time, because the enemy were so many.

Medicine Bear charged, and killed a man, and then came back, and the second time he charged the people charged all together, following him, and they killed many and drove the enemy off, and those who had the fastest horses were the only ones who got away. The Pawnees went home to the village.

Everybody rejoiced, and there were many scalp-dances. Now the poor boy was more highly thought of than ever. Even the chiefs bowed their heads when they saw him. They could not equal him. This time he called himself Ku ruks ti carish, Angry Bear.

After the excitement had quieted down, one day the head chief said: "Medicine Bear, in all this tribe there is no chief who is equal to you. Sit down by my daughter. Take her for your wife, and take my place as chief. I and my wife will go out of this lodge, and it shall be yours. You shall be the chief of the tribe. Whatever you say we will abide by." The poor boy said: "My father, I will think about this.

By morning I will let you know." In the night, before he slept, he filled the pipe and smoked as the Bear had told him to do, and then he went to bed. In dreams the Bear said to him: "My son, you have done what I wished you to do. Now the power will remain with you as long as you shall live. Now you can marry, if you will."

But the boy was not yet ready to do this. The girl was very pretty, and he liked her, but he felt that before he married there were still some things that he must do. He called his brother and said to him, "Go, kill the fattest of the buffalo; bring it to me, and I will take a long journey with you." His brother went hunting and killed a buffalo, and brought the meat home, and they dried it and made a bundle of it. Medicine Bear told his brother to carry this bundle and a rawhide rope and a little hatchet, and they started on a journey toward the Missouri River. One day toward evening they reached the river, and they found themselves on top of a steep-cut bluff. The river ran at its foot. The poor boy cut a cottonwood pole and drove it into the ground, and tied the rope to it, and then tied the other end of the rope about his brother's body.

Then he sharpened a stick and gave it to his brother and said: "Now take the bundle of meat, and I will let you down over the bank. You must put the meat on a ledge of the cliff, and when the birds come you must feed them. Give a piece to the first one that comes, and then take your sharp stick and get another piece, and so feed all the birds. They are the ones that have power, and they can take pity on you." So he let the chief's son down.

The first bird that came was a buzzard, then an eagle, then hawks and owls, all kinds of birds that kill their prey. He fed them all. While he was doing this, the poor boy was above lying on top of the bank. Late in the afternoon, just as the sun was going down, he saw, far up the river, what looked like a flock of geese coming. They came nearer and nearer, and at last passed out of sight under the bank.

Afterward, when he looked down on the river, he could see in the water red light as if it were all on fire, and as he lay on the bank he could hear down below him the sound of drumming and singing just as plain as could be, and all the time the chief's son was hanging there in front of the bank, and the poor boy would call down to him to cry and ask the animals to take pity on him. When Medicine Bear had done this, he started back and went home, leaving the chief's son hanging there.

The chief's son staid there all the night and all the next day, and for three days and nights, and on the night of the fourth day he fell asleep. When he awoke he was in a lodge. It was under the Missouri River. When he looked about him he saw that those in the lodge were all animals. There was the beaver, there was the otter, two buffalo, the antelope, hawks, owls, ermines, bears, frogs, woodpeckers, catfish -- all kinds of animals. On each side of the lodge was a little pool, and in each pool sat a goose, and every time they sang, the geese would shake their wings on the water, and it sounded just like drumming.

The chief of the animals spoke to him, saying: "My son, at this time we can do nothing for you. We must first send our messenger up to the Bear's lodge to ask him what we may do for you." While he was saying this the Bear's servant entered the lodge and said: "My father, it is all right. Our father the Bear told me to say to you that his son has sent this young man to you, and you must exert all your power for him."

Now the animals began to make ready to use their power to help the chief's son. First the Beaver talked to the young man, to tell him of his powers and his ways, so that he might perform wonderful acts. How he should take the branch of a tree and strike a man with its point and it would go through him, and then how to draw it out and to make the man well again. He gave him the power to do this. He taught him how to take a stick two feet long and swallow it, and then take it out again from his throat, and gave him this power.

The Otter gave him the power, if his enemies ever attacked him, to break their arrows with his teeth and shoot back the shaft without a spike, and if he hit an enemy with the shaft, it would kill him. "The poison from your mouth will kill him," he said.

The Ground-dog said: "My son, here is my little one. I give him to you. Take him, and if you have an enemy among the doctors in your tribe, take this little one down to the water early in the morning and dip his nose in the water, and when you take it out it will have a piece of liver in its mouth. The man who has tried to kill you will be found dead."

The Owl said: "My son, I give you power to see in the night. When you go on the warpath and want to take horses, the night will be like daytime for you."

The Hawk said: "My son, I give you power to run swiftly, and I give you my war-club, which is my wing. You shall strike your enemy with it only once, and the blow shall kill him. Take also this little black rope; you shall use it when you go on the war-path to catch horses. Take also this scalp which you see hanging down from my claw. You shall be a great man for scalping."

Each of the other animals gave him all his kinds of power.

For two days and two nights, they taught him the different kinds of power, and for two days and two nights they taught him the different kinds of roots and herbs for healing the sick. They said to him: "You shall be the great doctor of your people. Every now and then you must bring us tobacco, so that we can smoke."

They further told him that at this time they could teach him only a little, but that afterward, one at a time, they would meet him out on the prairie, and would teach him more. At last they said: "Now it is time for you to go. Your friend has come, and is waiting for you out on the prairie."

The Buffalo now stood up and said: "My son, I want to be with you always. I give you my robe. Wear it wherever you go, that the people may know that you come from this place." All the animals said, "We want to be with you too." Each one of the birds took off a feather and put it on the robe, and each animal put one of its claws on it, and some put medicine on it. In one of the holes the Beaver tied a little sweet-grass, and others did the same. By the time they were through, the robe was all covered with feathers and claws and smelt sweet. The animals had put their medicine on it so that it smelt sweet. Then the animals said, "Go, my son, to your people, and bring us something to smoke, so that we may be satisfied."

Presently the chief's son found himself upon the bluff, facing his brother. His brother grasped him in his arms and said: "Oh, my brother, you smell nice. What a fine robe you have on! Look at all these feathers." They hugged each other. Then they went home together. The chief's son had a bundle that the animals had given him.

Soon after this the Pawnees had a big doctors' dance. These boys went into the doctors' lodge and said: "Doctors, you are the head doctors, but we have come to-night to visit you. We want to do a few things ourselves." The doctors all said "Lau-a." The young men took seats close to the door, which is the most important place in this dance. All the doctors were surprised, and said "Uh!"

The Bear boy got up first and began shooting at the chief's son, just as he had done with the Bear, and all the doctors thought he was powerful, shooting at this young man and curing him. When he got through, it was the other boy's turn. He would take a long sharp stick and thrust it through his brother, and then heal him again, and then take a knife and stab him, and then cure him. He did some powerful things, more so than his brother had done. After the doctors had seen all these things they all said, "Let us have these two for our head doctors." But the poor boy said: "Not so. This one who is sitting by me has more power than I have. He ought to be the head doctor, for I am a warrior, and can never stay in the camp to doctor people. My brother has gone into the animals' lodge, and they have given him more power than I possess." So the chief's son was chosen to be the head doctor.

When the doctors' dance was over, the two brothers at once started to go to the animals' lodge, carrying with them tobacco and a pipe. When they got there, the chief's son told his brother to wait on the bank, that he was going down to take the tobacco and the pipe to his fathers.

He jumped off the steep bank into the river, down into the door of the lodge, and went in. When they saw him all the animals slapped their mouths and called out. They were glad to see him. After smoking with them, he went back to his friend. After that the chief's son would go off by himself and would meet the animals on the hills. They would tell him about different roots, and how to doctor this disease and that. He would come back with some roots and herbs and put them away.

Finally the head chief sent for the Bear man and said to him: "My son, I offered you my lodge, my daughter, and the whole tribe. Now take all this. Let me go out of this lodge and look for another one, and you stay here with my daughter." The young man said: "What of my brother? Send for the other chief. Let him give his daughter, his lodge, his people, to him, and this day we will accept your gifts to us. My brother will after this be the head doctor of this tribe." The other chief when asked to do this agreed, and it was so done.

The Bear man went often on the warpath, but his brother stayed at home, and fought against the enemy only when they attacked the village. He took charge of the doctors' lodge. The Bear man after this had some children, and when they had grown up he told his son the secrets of his power. He was now beginning to grow old, and his son went on the warpath, while he stayed at home.

One night he had a dream about his father the Bear. The Bear said to him: "My son, I made you great and powerful among your people. The hairs of my body are falling and soon I shall die. Then you too will die. Tell your son all the secret powers that I gave you. He shall keep the same power that you have had."

Soon after this the old Bear must have died, for the man died. Before he died he said to his brother: "Do not mourn for me, for I shall always be near you. Take care of your people. Cure them when they are sick, and always be their chief."

When the enemy came and attacked these people and wounded any, the chief's son was always there and always cured them. He was a great doctor. At last he also died, but his son had the same kind of power. But these two sons never had so great a power as their fathers.

A Little Brave and the Medicine Woman

A Sioux Legend
Marie L. McLaughlin,
Myths and Legends of the Sioux, 1913

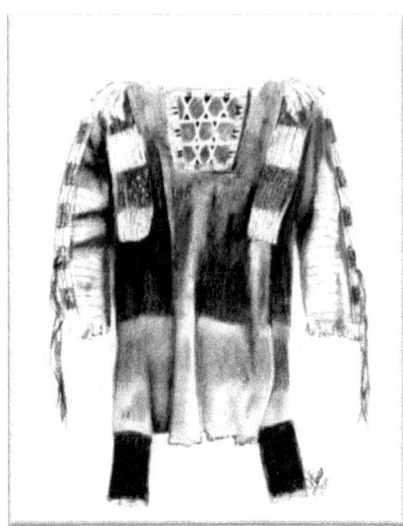

A village of Indians moved out of winter camp and pitched their tents in a circle on high land overlooking a lake. A little way down the hill was a grave. Choke cherries had grown up, hiding the grave from view. But as the ground had sunk somewhat, the grave was marked by a slight hollow.

One of the villagers going out to hunt took a short cut through the choke cherry bushes. As he pushed them aside he saw the hollow grave, but thought it was a washout made by the rains.

But as he moved to step over it, to his great surprise he stumbled and fell. Made curious by his mishap, he drew back and tried again; but again he fell. When he came back to the village he told the old men what had happened to him.

They remembered then that a long time before there had been buried there a medicine woman or conjurer. Doubtless it was her medicine that made him stumble.

The story of the villager's adventure spread thru the camp and made many curious to see the grave. Among others were six little boys who were, however, rather timid, for they were in great awe of the dead medicine woman.

But they had a little playmate named Brave, a mischievous little rogue, whose hair was always unkempt and tossed about and who was never quiet for a moment.

"Let us ask Brave to go with us," they said. And they went as a group to see him.

"All right," said Brave; "I will go with you. But I have something to do first. You go on around the hill that way, and I will hasten around this way, and meet you a little later near the grave."

So the six little boys went on as bidden until they came to a place near the grave. There they halted.

"Where is Brave?" they asked.

Now Brave, full of mischief, had thought to play a joke on his little friends. As soon as they were well out of sight he had sped around the hill to the shore of the lake and sticking his hands in the mud had rubbed it over his face, plastered it in his hair, and soiled his hands until he looked like a new risen corpse with the flesh rotting from his bones. He then went and lay down in the grave and awaited the boys.

When the six little boys came they were more timid than ever when they did not find Brave; but they feared to go back to the village without seeing the grave, for fear the old men would call them cowards.

So they slowly approached the grave and one of them timidly called out, "Please, grandmother, we won't disturb your grave. We only want to see where you lie. Don't be angry."

At once a thin quavering voice, like an old woman's, called out, "Han, han, takoja, hechetuya, hechetuya! Yes, yes, that's right, that's right."

The boys were frightened out of their senses, believing the old woman had come to life.

"Oh, grandmother," they gasped, "don't hurt us; please don't, we'll go."

Just then Brave raised his muddy face and hands up thru the choke cherry bushes. With the oozy mud dripping from his features he looked like some very witch just raised from the grave. The boys screamed outright. One fainted. The rest ran yelling up the hill to the village, where each broke at once for his mother's teepee.

As all the tents in a Dakota camping circle face the center, the boys as they came tearing into camp were in plain view from the teepees. Hearing the screaming, every woman in camp ran to her teepee door to see what had happened. Just then little Brave, as badly scared as the rest, came rushing in after them, his hair on end and covered with mud and crying out, all forgetful of his appearance, "It's me, it's me!"

The women yelped and bolted in terror from the village. Brave dashed into his mother's teepee, scaring her out of her wits. Dropping pots and kettles, she tumbled out of the tent to run screaming with the rest. Not a single villager come near poor little Brave until he had gone down to the lake and washed himself

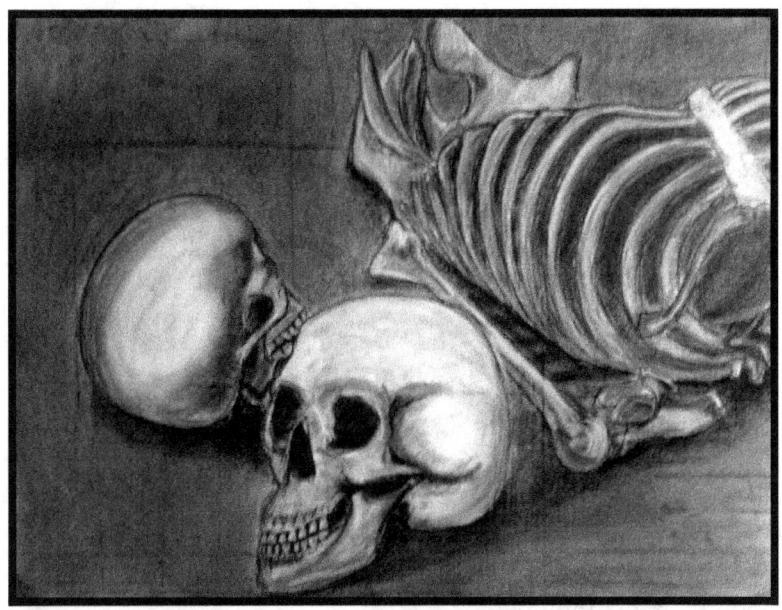

The Man Who Was Afraid of Nothing

Brule Sioux
Told by Lame Deer, and recorded by Richard Erdoes.

Now, there were four ghosts sitting together, talking, smoking ghost smoke, having a good time, as far as it's possible for ghosts to have a good time. One of them said: "I've heard of a young man nothing can scare. He's not afraid of us, so they say."

The second ghost said: "I bet I could scare him." The third ghost said: "We must try to make him shiver and run and hide." The fourth ghost said: "Let's bet; let's make a wager. Whoever can scare him the most, wins." And they agreed to bet their ghost horses.

So this young man who was never afraid came walking along one night. The moon was shining. Suddenly in his path the first ghost materialized, taking the form of a skeleton. "Hou, friend," said the ghost, clicking his teeth together, making a sound like a water drum.

"Hou, cousin," said the young man, "you're in my way. Get off the road and let me pass." "Not until we have played the hoop-and-stick game. If you lose, I'll make you into a skeleton like me."

The young man laughed. He bent the skeleton into a big hoop, tying it with some grass. He took one of the skeleton's leg bones for his game stick and rolled the skeleton along, scoring again and again with the leg bone. "Well, I guess I won this game," said the young man. "How about some shinny ball?"

The young man took the skeleton's skull and used the leg bone to drive it ahead of him like a ball.

"Ouch!" said the skull. "You're hurting me; you're giving me a headache."

"Well, you asked for it. Who proposed this game, you or me? You're a silly fellow." The young man kicked the skull aside and walked on.

Further on he met the second ghost also in the form of a skeleton, who jumped at him and grabbed him with bony hands. "Let's dance, friend," the skeleton said.

"A very good idea, cousin ghost," said the young man. "What shall we use for a drum and drumstick? I know!" Taking the ghost's thighbone and skull, the young man danced and sang, beating on the skull with the bone.

"Stop, stop!" cried the skull. "This is no way to dance. You're hurting me; you're giving me a headache."

"You're lying, ghost," said the young man. "Ghosts can't feel pain."

"I don't know about other ghosts," said the skull, "but me, I'm hurting."

"For a ghost you're awfully sensitive," said the young man. "Really, I'm disappointed. There we were, having a good time, and you spoiled my fun with your whining. Groan somewhere else."

The young man kicked the skull aside and scattered the rest of the bones all over.

"Now see what you've done," complained the ghost, "it will take me hours to get all my bones together. You're a bad man." "Stop your whining," said the young man. "It gives you something to do." Then he went on. Soon he came upon the third ghost, another skeleton. "This is getting monotonous," said the young man. "Are you the same as before? Did I meet you further back?"

"No," Said the ghost. "Those were my cousins. They're soft. I'm tough. Let's wrestle. If I win, I'll make you into a skeleton like me."

"My friend," said the young man, "I don't feel like wrestling with you, I feel like sledding. There's enough snow on the hill for that. I should have buffalo ribs for it, but your rib cage will go."

The young man took the ghost's rib cage and used it as a sled. "This is fun!" he said, whizzing down the hill.

"Stop, stop," cried the ghost's skull "You're breaking my ribs!"

The young man said: "Friend, you look funny without a rib cage. You've grown so short. Here!" And he threw the ribs into a stream. "Look what you've done! What can I do without my ribs? I need them."

"Jump in the water and dive for them," said the young man. "You look as if you need a bath. It'll do you good, and your woman will appreciate it."

'What do you mean? I am a woman!" said the ghost, insulted.

"With skeletons I can't tell, you pretty thing," he said, and walked on.

Then he came upon the chief ghost, a skeleton riding a skeleton horse. "I've come to kill you," said the skeleton. The young man made faced at the ghost. He rolled his eyes; he showed his teeth; he gnashed them; he made weird noises. "I'm a ghost myself, a much more terrible ghost than you are," he said.

The skeleton got scared and tried to turn his ghost horse, but the young man seized it by the bridle. "A horse is just what I want," he said. 'I've walked enough. Get off!" He yanked the skeleton from its mount and broke it into pieces. The skeleton was whimpering, but the young man mounted the skeleton horse and rode it into camp. Day was just breaking, and some women who were up early to get water saw him and screamed loudly. They ran away while the whole village was awakened by their shrieking. The people looked out of their tipis and became frightened when they saw him on the ghost horse. As soon as the sun appeared, however, the skeleton vanished. The young man laughed.

The story of his ride on the skeleton horse was told all through the camp. Later he joined a group of men and started to brag about putting the four skeleton ghosts to flight. People shook their heads, saying, "This young man is really brave. Nothing frightens him. He is the bravest man who ever lived."

Just then a tiny spider was crawling up this young man's sleeve. When someone called his attention to it, he cried, "Eeeeech! Get this bug off me! Please, someone take it off, I can't stand spiders! Eeeeeeech!" He shivered, he writhed, he carried on. A little girl laughed and took the spider off him.

The Ghosts' Buffalo
A Blackfoot Legend

A long time ago there were four Blackfeet, who went to war against the Crees. They traveled a long way, and at last their horses gave out, and they started back toward their homes. As they were going along they came to the Sand Hills; and while they were passing through them, they saw in the sand a fresh travois trail, where people had been travelling.

One of the men said: "Let us follow this trail until we come up with some of our people. Then we will camp with them." They followed the trail for a long way, and at length one of the Blackfeet, named E-kus'-kini, a very powerful person, said to the others: "Why follow this longer? It is just nothing." The others said: "Not so. These are our people. We will go on and camp with them." They went on, and toward evening, one of them found a stone maul and a dog travois. He said: "Look at these things. I know this maul and this travois. They belonged to my mother, who died. They were buried with her. This is strange." He took the things. When night overtook the men, they camped.

Early in the morning, they heard, all about them, sounds as if a camp of people were there. They heard a young man shouting a sort of war cry, as young men do; women chopping wood; a man calling for a feast, asking people to come to his lodge and smoke, all the different sounds of the camp. They looked about, but could see nothing; and then they were frightened and covered their heads with their robes. At last they took courage, and started to look around and see what they could learn about this strange thing. For a little while they saw nothing, but pretty soon one of them said: "Look over there. See that pis'kun. Let us go over and look at it." As they were going toward it, one of them picked up a stone pointed arrow. He said: "Look at this. It belonged to my father. This is his place." They started to go on toward the pis'kun, but suddenly they could see no pis'kun. It had disappeared all at once.

A little while after this, one of them spoke up, and said: "Look over there. There is my father running buffalo. There! he has killed. Let us go over to him." They all looked where this man pointed, and they could see a person on a white horse, running buffalo. While they were looking, the person killed the buffalo, and got off his horse to butcher it. They started to go over toward him, and saw him at work butchering, and saw him turn the buffalo over on its back; but before they got to the place where he was, the person got on his horse and rode off, and when they got to where he had been skinning the buffalo, they saw lying on the ground only a dead mouse. There was no buffalo there. By the side of the mouse was a buffalo chip, and lying on it was an arrow painted red. The man said: "That is my father's arrow. That is the way he painted them." He took it up in his hands; and when he held it in his hands, he saw that it was not an arrow but a blade of spear grass. Then he laid it down, and it was an arrow again.

Another Blackfoot found a buffalo rock, I-nis'-kim.

Some time after this, the men got home to their camp. The man who had taken the maul and the dog travois, when he got home and smelled the smoke from the fire, died, and so did his horse. It seems that the shadow of the person who owned the things was angry at him and followed him home. Two others of these Blackfeet have since died, killed in war; but E-kus'-kini is alive yet. He took a stone and an iron arrow point that had belonged to his father, and always carried them about with him. That is why he has lived so long. The man who took the stone arrow point found near the pis'kun, which had belonged to his father, took it home with him. This was his medicine. After that he was badly wounded in two fights, but he was not killed; he got well.

The one who took the buffalo rock, I-nis'-kim, it afterward made strong to call the buffalo into the pis'kun. He would take the rock and put it in his lodge close to the fire, where he could look at it, and would pray over it and make medicine. Sometimes he would ask for a hundred buffalo to jump into the pis'kun, and the next day a hundred would jump in. He was powerful.

The Land of the Dead

Serrano
From a story reported by Ruth Benedict in 1926

A great hunter brought home a wife. They loved each other and were very happy. But the man's mother hated the young wife, and one day when the husband was out hunting, she put a sharp, pointed object in the wife's seat, and the woman sat down upon it and was killed.

The people immediately brought brush and piled it up. They put her body on it and burned it, and by the time her husband returned that night her body was consumed.

The man went to the burning place and stayed there motionless. Curls of dust rose and whirled about the charred spot. He watched them all night and all day. At evening they grew larger, and at last one larger than all the rest whirled round and round the burned spot. It set off down the road and he set off after it. When it was quite dark, he saw that the dust he was following was his wife, but she would not speak to him.

She was leading him in the direction of the rock past which all dead people go. If they have lived bad lives, the rock falls on them and crushes them. When they came to it, she spoke to her husband. "We are going to the place of dead people," she told him. "I will take you on my back so that you will not be seen and recognized as one of the living."

Thus they traveled on until they came to the river that the dead have to ford. This was very dangerous for the man because he was not dead, but the woman kept him on her back, and they came through safely. The woman went directly to her people, to her parents and brothers and sisters who had died before. They were glad to see her, but they did not like the man, for he was not dead. The woman pleaded for him, however, and they let him stay. Special food always had to be cooked for him, because he could not eat what dead people live on. And in the daytime he could see nothing, it was as if he were alone all day long; only in the night did he see his wife and the other people.

When the dead were going hunting, they took him along and stationed him on the trail the deer would take. Presently he heard them shouting, "The deer, the deer!" and he knew they were shouting to him that the deer were coming in his direction. But he could see nothing. Then he looked again and spotted two little black beetles, which he knocked over. When the people had come up, they praised him for his hunting.

After that the dead did not complain about his presence, but they did feel sorry for him. "It's not time for him to die yet," they said. "He has a hard time here. The woman ought to go back with him." So they arranged for both of them to return, and they instructed the man and the woman to have nothing to do with each other for three nights after they were back on earth.

Three nights for the dead, however, meant three years for the living. Not aware of this, the husband and wife returned to earth and remained continent for three nights. The following evening, they embraced, and when the husband woke on the morning of the fourth day, he was alone.

Blue Jay Visits Ghost Town

Chinook
Based on a tale reported by Franz Boas in 1894.

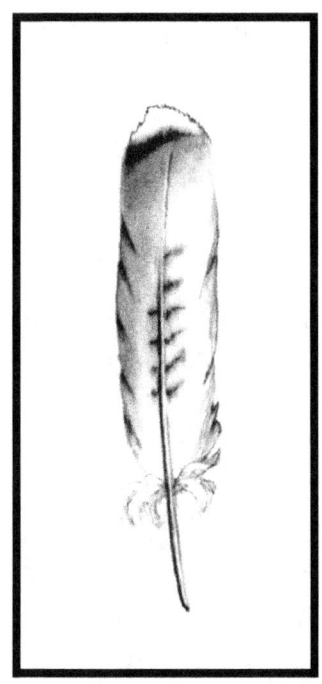

One night the ghosts decided to go out and buy a wife. They chose a woman named Io'i, and gave her family dentalia as a dowry. They were married one night, and on the following morning Io'i disappeared.

Now Io'i had a brother named Blue Jay. For a year he waited to hear from her, then said, "I'll go and search for her." He asked all the trees, "Where do people go when they die?" They remained silent. He asked all the birds, but they did not tell him either. Then he asked an old wedge. It said, "Pay me and I'll carry you there." He did, and it took him to the ghosts.

The wedge and Blue Jay arrived near a large town, where they saw no smoke rising from any of the houses except the last one, a great edifice. Blue Jay went into it and found his elder sister, who greeted him fondly.

"Ah, my brother," she said, "where have you come from? Have you died?" "Oh, no," he said, "I am not dead at all. The wedge brought me here on his back." Then he went out and opened the doors to all the other houses. They were full of bones. He noticed a skull and bones lying near his sister, and when he asked her what she was doing with them, she replied: "That's your brother-in-law." "Pshaw! Io'i is lying all the time," he thought. "She says a skull is my brother-in-law!" But when it grew dark people arose from what had been just bones, and the house was suddenly full of activity.

When Blue Jay asked his sister about all the people, she laughed and replied, "Do you think they are people? These are ghosts!" Even hearing this, though, he resumed staying with his sister. She said to him, "Do as they do and go fishing with your dip net." "I think I will,". he replied. "Go with that boy," she said, pointing to a figure. "He is one of your brother-in-Iaw's relations. But don't speak to him; keep quiet." These people always spoke in whispers, so that Blue Jay didn't understand them.

And so they started in their canoes. He and his guide caught up with a crowd of people who were going down the river, singing aloud as they paddled. When Blue Jay joined their song, they fell silent. Blue Jay looked back and saw that where the boy had been, there were now only bones in the stern of the canoe. They continued to go down the river, and Blue Jay kept quiet. Then he looked at the stern again, and the boy was sitting there. Blue Jay said in a low voice, "Where is your fish trap?" He spoke slowly, and the boy replied, "It's down the river." They paddled on. Then Blue Jay said in a loud voice, "Where is your trap?" This time he found only a skeleton in the stern. Blue Jay was again silent. He looked back, and the boy was sitting in the canoe. He lowered his voice and said, "Where is your trap?" "Here," replied the boy.

Now they fished with their dip nets. Blue Jay felt something in his net, lifted it, and found only two branches. He turned his net and threw them into the water. When he put his net again into the water, it soon became full of leaves. He threw them back, but some fell into the canoe and the boy gathered them up. Then Blue Jay caught another branch and some more leaves and threw them back; but again a few leaves fell into the canoe, and again the boy gathered them up. As they continued fishing, Blue Jay caught two more branches that he decided to take back to Io'i for making a fire.

They arrived at home and went up to the house. Blue Jay was angry that he had not caught anything, but the boy brought up a mat full of trout, even though Blue Jay had not seen him catch a single one in his net. While the people were roasting them, the boy announced, "He threw most of the catch out of the canoe. Our canoe would have been full if he had not thrown so much away." His sister said to Blue Jay: "Why did you throw away what you had caught?" "I threw away nothing but branches and leaves." "That is our food," she replied. "Did you think they were branches? The leaves were trout, and the branches were fall salmon." He said, "Well, I brought you two branches to use for making a fire." So his sister went down to the beach and found two fall salmon in the canoe. She carried them up to the house, and Blue Jay said, "Where did you steal those salmon?" She replied, "That's what you caught." "Io'i is always lying," Blue Jay said.

The next day Blue Jay went to the beach. There lay the canoes of the ghosts, now full of holes and covered with moss. He went up to the house and said to his sister, "How bad your husband's canoes are, Io'i!" "Oh, be quiet," she said. "They'll become tired of you." "But the canoes of these people are full of holes!" Exasperated, his sister turned to him and said, "Are they people? Are they people? Don't you understand? They are ghosts."

When it grew dark again, Blue Jay and the boy made themselves ready to go fishing again. This time he teased the boy: as they made their way down the river, he would shout, and only bones would be there. When they began fishing, Blue Jay gathered in the branches and leaves instead of throwing them away. When the ebb tide set in, their canoe was full. On the way home, he teased all the other ghosts. As soon as they met one he would shout out loud, and only bones would lie in the other canoe. They arrived at home, and he presented his sister with armfuls of fall salmon and silver-side salmon.

The next morning Blue Jay went into the town and waited for the dark, when the life came back. That evening he heard someone announce, "Ah, a whale has been found!" His sister gave him a knife and said, "Run! a whale has been found!" Anxious to gather meat, Blue Jay ran to the beach, but when he met one of the people and asked in a loud voice, "Where is the whale?" only a skeleton lay there. He kicked the skull and left it. A few yards away he met some other people, but again he shouted loudly, and again only skeletons lay there. Then he came to a large log with thick bark. A crowd of people were peeling off the bark, and Blue Jay shouted to them so that only skeletons lay there. The bark was full of pitch. He peeled off two pieces and carried them home on his shoulder.

He went home and threw the bark down outside the house. He said to his sister, "I really thought it was a whale. Look here: it's just bark from a fir." His sister said, "It's whale meat, it's whale meat; did you think it's just bark?" His sister went out and pointed to two cuts of whale meat lying on the ground. "It's good whale, and its blubber is very thick." Blue Jay stared down at the bark, astonished to find a dead whale lying there. Then he turned back, and when he saw a person carrying a piece of bark on his back, he shouted and nothing but a skeleton lay there. He grabbed the bark and carried it home, then went back to catch more ghosts. In the course of time he had many meals of whale meat.

The next morning, he entered a house and took a child's skull, which he put on a large skeleton. And he took a large skull and put it on that child's skeleton. He mixed up all the people like this, and when it grew dark the child rose to its feet. It wanted to sit up, but it fell down again because its head pulled it down. The old man arose. His head was too light! The next morning Blue Jay replaced the heads and switched around their legs instead. He gave small legs to an old man, and large legs to a child. Sometimes he exchanged a man's and a woman's legs.

In course of time Blue Jay's antics began to make him very unpopular. Io'i's husband said: "Tell him he must go home. He mistreats them, and these people don't like him." Io'i tried to stop her younger brother's pranks, but he would pay no attention. On the next morning he awoke early and found Io'i holding a skull in her arms. He tossed it away and asked, "Why do you hold that skull, Io'i? "Ah, you have broken your brother-in-law's neck!" When it grew dark, his brother-in-law was gravely sick, but a shaman was able to make him well again.

Finally, Blue Jay decided it was time to go home. His sister gave him five buckets full of water and said, "Take care! When you come to burning prairies, save the water until you come to the fourth prairie. Then pour it out." "All right," replied Blue Jay. He started out and reached a prairie. It was hot. Red flowers bloomed on the prairie. He poured water on the prairie, using half of one of his buckets. He passed through a woods and reached another prairie, which was burning at its end. "This is what my sister told me about." He poured the rest of the bucket out on the trail. He took another bucket and poured, and when it was half empty he reached the woods on the other side of the prairie. He came to still another prairie, the third one. One half of it was burning strongly. He took a bucket and emptied it. He took another bucket and emptied half of it.

Then he reached the woods on the other side of the prairie.

Now he had only two and a half buckets left. He came to another prairie which was almost totally on fire. He took the half bucket and emptied it. He took one more bucket, and when he arrived at the woods at the far side of the prairie, he had emptied it. Now only one bucket was left. He reached another prairie which was completely ablaze. He eked out the last drop of water.

When he had gotten nearly across he had run out of water, so he took off his bearskin blanket and beat the fire. The whole bearskin blanket blazed up. Then his head and his hair caught fire and soon Blue Jay himself was burned to death.

Now when it was just growing dark Blue Jay returned to his sister. "Kukukukukuku, Io'i," he called. Mournfully his sister cried, "Ah, my brother is dead." His trail led to the water on the other side of the river. She launched her canoe to fetch him. Io'i's canoe seemed beautiful to him.

She said, "And you told me that my canoe was moss-grown!" "Ah, Io'i is always telling lies. The other ones had holes and were moss-grown, anyway." "You are dead now, Blue Jay, so you see things differently." But still he insisted, "Io'i is always telling lies."

Now she paddled her brother across to the other side. He saw the people. Some sang; some played dice with beaver teeth or with ten disks. The women played hoops. Farther along, Blue Jay heard people singing conjurers' songs and saw them dancing, kumm, kumm, kumm, kumm. He tried to sing and shout, but they all laughed at him.

Blue Jay entered his sister's house and saw that his brother-in-law was a chief, and a handsome one. She said, "And you broke his neck!" "Io'i is always telling lies. Where did these canoes come from? They're pretty." "And you said they were all moss-grown!" "Io'i is always telling lie.

The others all had holes. Parts of them were moss-grown." "You are dead now, and you see things differently," said his sister. "Io'i is always telling lies." Blue Jay tried to shout at the people, but they laughed at him. Then he gave it up and became quiet. Later when his sister went to look for him, he was standing near the dancing conjurors. He wanted their powers, but they only laughed at him. He pestered them night after night, and after five nights he came back to his sister's house. She saw him dancing on his head, his legs upward. She turned back and cried. Now he had really died. He had died a second time, made witless by the magicians.

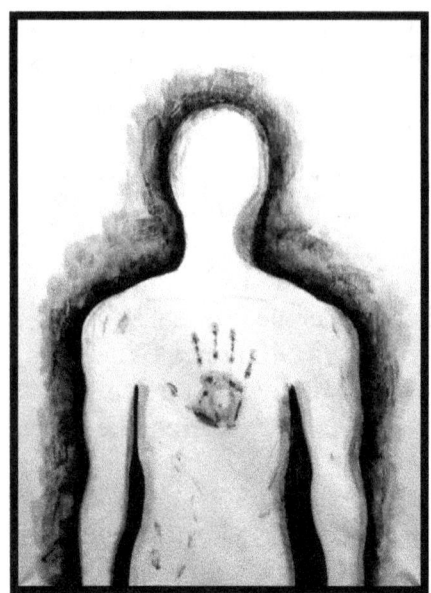

The Spirit Land

*A Gallinomero Legend
Katharine Berry Judson, Myths and Legends of California and the Old Southwest, 1912*

When the flames burn low on the funeral pyres of the Gallinomero, Indian mourners gather up handfuls of ashes and scatter them high in air. Thus the good mount up into the air, or go to the Happy Western Land beyond the Big Water.

But the bad Indians go to an island in the Bitter Waters, an island naked and barren and desolate, covered only with brine-spattered stone, swept with cold winds and the biting sea-spray.

Here they live always, breaking stone upon one another, with no food but the broken stones and no drink but the salt sea water.

The Skin Shifting Old Woman

*A Wichita Legend
Dorsey,
Publications of the
Carnegie Institution, xxi, 124, No. 17*

In the story of Healthy-Flint-Stone-Man, it is told that he was a powerful man and lived in a village and was a chief of the place. He was not a man of heavy build, but was slim.

Often when a man is of this type of build he is called "Healthy-Flint-Stone-Man," after the man in the story. Healthy-Flint-Stone-Man had parents, but at this time he had no wife. Soon afterwards he married, and his wife was the prettiest woman that ever lived in the village. When she married Healthy-Flint-Stone-Man they lived at his home.

She was liked by his parents, for she was a good worker and kind-hearted. As was their custom, the men of the village came at night to visit Healthy-Flint-Stone-Man, and his wife did the cooking to feed them, so that he liked her all the more, and was kind to her.

Early in the morning a strange woman by the name of Little-Old-Woman came to their place and asked the wife to go with her to get wood. Out of kindness to Little-Old-Woman she went with her, leaving her husband at home. Little-Old-Woman knew where all the dry wood was to be found. When they reached the place where she thought there was plenty of wood they did not stop.

They went on past, although there was plenty of good dry wood. The wife began to cut wood for the old woman and some for herself. When she had cut enough for both she fixed it into two bundles, one for each. Little-Old-Woman knelt by her pile and waited for the wife to help her up. Little-Old-Woman then helped the wife in the same way, and they started toward their home.

They talked on the way about their manner of life at home. Arrived at the village, the old woman went to her home. When the wife got home she began to do her work.

Again, the second time, the old woman came around and asked the wife to go with her to fetch wood. They started away together, and this time went farther than on the first time to get their wood, though they passed much good wood. The wife cut wood for both and arranged it in two piles, but this time she herself first knelt by her pile and asked the old woman to take hold of her hands and pull her up; then the wife helped the old woman with her load.

They returned home, and on the way the old woman said to the wife, "If you will go with me to fetch wood for the fourth time I shall need no more help from you." They again went far beyond where any other women had gone to get wood. When they got to the village they parted. The wife wondered why the old woman came to her for help. She found the men passing the time talking of the past as usual. She kept on doing her duty day after day.

The third time the old woman came for the wife to ask her to help her fetch wood, as she was all out of it again. Again they went out, and this time they went still further for the wood, and now they were getting a long way from the village. The wife cut wood and arranged it in two bundles, one for each of them to carry. This time it was the old woman's turn first to be helped up with the wood.

They helped each other, and on the way home the old woman told the wife that they had only once more to go for wood, and the work would all be done. She always seemed thankful for the help she received. They reached the village and went to their homes. The wife found her men as usual, and commenced to do her work. After the men were through eating they went home, though some stayed late in the night.

Finally, the old woman came the fourth time to ask the wife to go with her and help her fetch some wood. This time they went about twice as far as they had gone the third time from the village. When the old woman thought they were far enough they stopped, and the wife began cutting wood for both of them. When she had cut enough she arranged it in two bundles. Now it was the wife's turn to be helped up with the wood, but the old woman refused to do it as usual and told her to go ahead and kneel by the bundle of wood. The wife refused.

Now, each tried to persuade the other to kneel first against the bundle of wood. The old woman finally prevailed, and the wife knelt against the wood, and as she put her robe around her neck the old woman seemed pleased to help her, but as the old woman was fixing the carrying ropes she tightened them, after slipping them around the wife's neck until the wife fell at full length, as though dying.

The old woman sat down to rest, as she was tired from choking the wife. Soon she got up and untied the wife. Now, they were in the thick timber, and there was flowing water through it.

After the old woman had killed the wife she blew into the top of her head and blew the skin from her, hair and all. This she did because she envied the wife her good looks, since the wife was the best-looking woman in the village, and her husband was good-looking and well thought of by all the prominent men, and the old woman wanted to be treated as well as the wife had been treated.

Then the old woman began to put on the wife's skin, but the wife was a little smaller than the old woman, though the old woman managed to stretch the skin and drew it over her, fitting herself to it. Then she smoothed down the skin until it fitted her nicely. She took the wife's body to the flowing water and threw it in, having found a place that was never visited by anyone, and that had no trail leading to it. She then went to her pile of wood and took it to her home. She found the men visiting the chief.

The chief did not discover that she was not his wife. The old woman knew all about the former wife's ways, for she had talked much with her when they were coming home with the wood, and she had asked the wife all sorts of questions about her husband. She understood how the men carried on at the chief's place. The wife had told the chief that the old woman had said that they were to go for wood four different times, and the last time being the fourth time, he supposed it was all over and his wife had got through with the old woman. So, as the old woman was doing his wife's duty, he thought her to be his wife until the time came when the skin began to decay and the hair to come off. Still there were big crowds of men around, and the old woman began to be fearful lest they would find her out.

So she made as if she were sick. The chief tried to get a man to doctor her, but she refused to be doctored. Finally, he hired a servant to doctor her. This was the man who always sat right by the entrance, ready to do errands or carry announcements to the people. His name was Buffalo-Crow-Man. He had a dark complexion. The old woman began to rave at his medicine working.

He began to tell who the old woman was, saying that there was no need of doctoring her; that she was a fraud and an evil spirit; and that she had become the wife of the chief through her bad deeds. The old woman told the chief not to believe the servant; and that he himself was a fraud and was trying to get her to do something wrong. The servant then stood at the feet of the old woman and began to sing.

Then over her body he went and jumped at her head. Then he commenced to sing again, first on her left side, then on her right. He sang the song four times, and while he was doing this the decayed hide came off from her. The servant told the men to take her out and take her life for what she had done to the chief's wife, telling how she had fooled the chief. They did as they were told.

The servant told the men he had suspected the old woman when she had come around to get the wife to go after wood with her; that when going after wood they always went a long distance, so that no one could observe them, but that he had always flown very high over them, so they could not see him, and had watched them; that on the fourth time they went for wood he had seen the old woman choke the wife with the wife's rope; how the old woman had secured the whole skin of the wife and had thrown her body into the flowing water. He told the men where the place was, and directed them there the next day. The men went to their homes, feeling very sad for the wicked thing the old woman had done.

On the next day the chief went as directed, and he came to

a place where he found a pile of wood that belonged to his former wife. He went to the place where he supposed his wife to be. He sat down and commenced to weep. There he stayed all night and the next day. He returned to his home, but he could not forget the occurrence. So he went back again and stayed another night and again returned home.

The chief was full of sorrow. He went back to the place the third time, and when he got there he sat down and commenced to weep. Again he stayed all night, and early next morning it was foggy and he could not see far. While he sat and wept he faced the east, and he was on the west side of the flowing waters, so that he also faced the flowing water wherein his wife's body was thrown.

He heard some one singing, but he was unable to catch the sound so that he could locate the place where the sound came from. He finally discovered that it came from the flowing water. He went toward the place and listened, and indeed it was his wife's voice, and this is what she sang: Woman-Having-Powers-in-the-Water, Woman-Having-Powers-in-the-Water, I am the one (you seek), I am here in the water.

As he went near the river he saw in the middle of the water his wife standing on the water. She told him to go back home and tell his parents to clean their grass-lodge and to purify the room by burning sage. She told her husband that he might then return and take her home; that he should tell his parents not to weep when she should return, but that they should rejoice at her return to life, and that after that he could take her home. So the man started to his home.

After he arrived he told his mother to clean and purify the lodge; and that he had found his wife and that he was going back again to get her. He told her that neither she nor any of their friends should weep at sight of the woman. While his mother was doing this cleaning he went back to the river and stayed one more night, and early in the morning he heard the woman singing again. He knew that he was to bring his wife back to his home. When he heard her sing he went straight to her.

She came out of the water and he met her. She began to tell her husband about her troubles--how she met troubles and how he was deceived. That day they went to their home, and Flint-Stone-Man's parents were glad to see his wife back once more. They lived together until long afterward.

The Spirit Wife

Zuni
Retold from a nineteenth-century version.

A young man was grieving because the beautiful young wife whom he loved was dead. As he sat at the graveside weeping, he decided to follow her to the Land of the Dead. He made many prayer sticks and sprinkled sacred corn pollen. He took a downy eagle plume and colored it with red earth color. He waited until nightfall, when the spirit of his departed wife came out of the grave and sat beside him. She was not sad, but smiling. The spirit-maiden told her husband: "I am just leaving one life for another. Therefore, do not weep for me."

"I cannot let you go," said the young man, "I love you so much that I will go with you to the land of the dead."

The spirit-wife tried to dissuade him, but could not overcome his determination. So at last she gave in to his wishes, saying: "If you must follow me, know that I shall be invisible to you as long as the sun shines. You must tie this red eagle plume to my hair. It will be visible in daylight, and if you want to come with me, you must follow the plume."

The young husband tied the red plume to his spirit-wife's hair, and at daybreak, as the sun slowly began to light up the world, bathing the mountaintops in a pale pink light, the spirit-wife started to fade from his view. The lighter it became, the more the form of his wife dissolved and grew transparent, until at last it vanished altogether. But the red plume did not disappear. It waved before the young man, a mere arm's length away, and then, as if rising and falling on a dancer's head, began leading the way out of the village, moving through the streets out into the cornfields, moving through a shallow stream, moving into the foothills of the mountains, leading the young husband ever westward toward the land of the evening.

The red plume moved swiftly, evenly, floating without effort over the roughest trails, and soon the young man had trouble following it. He grew more and more tired and finally was totally exhausted as the plume left him farther behind. Then he called out, panting: "Beloved wife, wait for me. I can't run any longer."

The red plume stopped, waiting for him to catch up, and when he did so, hastened on. For many days the young man traveled, following the plume by day, resting during the nights, when his spirit-bride would sometimes appear to him, speaking encouraging words. Most of the time, however, he was merely aware of her presence in some mysterious way. Day by day the trail became rougher and rougher. The days were long, the nights short, and the young man grew wearier and wearier, until at last he had hardly enough strength to set one foot before the other.

One day the trail led to a deep, almost bottomless chasm, and as the husband came to its edge, the red plume began to float away from him into nothingness. He reached out to seize it, but the plume was already beyond his reach, floating straight across the canyon, because spirits can fly through the air.

The young man called across the chasm: "Dear wife of mine, I love you. Wait!"

He tried to descend one side of the canyon, hoping to climb up the opposite side, but the rock walls were sheer, with nothing to hold onto. Soon he found himself on a ledge barely wider than a thumb, from which he could go neither forward nor back. It seemed that he must fall into the abyss and be dashed into pieces. His foot had already begun to slip, when a tiny striped squirrel scooted up the cliff, chattering: "You young fool, do you think you have the wings of a bird or the feet of a spirit? Hold on for just a little while and I'll help you." The little creature reached into its cheek pouch and brought out a little seed, which it moistened with saliva and stuck into a crack in the wall. With his tiny feet the squirrel danced above the crack, singing: "Tsithl, tsithl, tsithl, tall stalk, tall stalk, tall stalk, sprout, sprout quickly." Out of the crack sprouted a long, slender stalk, growing quickly in length and breadth, sprouting leaves and tendrils, spanning the chasm so that the young man could cross over without any trouble.

On the other side of the canyon, the young man found the red plume waiting, dancing before him as ever. Again he followed it at a pace so fast that it often seemed that his heart would burst. At last the plume led him to a large, dark, deep lake, and the plume plunged into the water to disappear below the surface. Then the husband knew that the spirit land lay at the bottom of the lake. He was in despair because he could not follow the plume into the deep. In vain did he call for his spirit-wife to come back. The surface of the lake remained undisturbed and unruffled like a sheet of mica. Not even at night did his spirit-wife reappear. The lake, the land of the dead, had swallowed her up. As the sun rose above the mountains, the young man buried his face in his hands and wept.

Then he heard someone gently calling: "Hu-hu-hu," and felt the soft beating of wings on his back and shoulders. He looked up and saw an owl hovering above him. The owl said: "Young man, why are you weeping?"

He pointed to the lake, saying: "My beloved wife is down there in the land of the dead, where I cannot follow her."

"I know, poor man," said the owl. "Follow me to my house in the mountains, where I will tell you what to do. If you follow my advice, all will be well and you will be reunited with the one you love."

The owl led the husband to a cave in the mountains and, as they entered, the young man found himself in a large room full of owl-men and owl-women. The owls greeted him warmly, inviting him to sit down and rest, to eat and drink. Gratefully he took his seat.

The old owl who had brought him took his owl clothing off, hanging it on an antler jutting out from the wall, and revealed himself as a man-like spirit. From a bundle in the wall this mysterious being took a small bag, showing it to the young man, telling him: "I will give this to you, but first I must instruct you in what you must do and must not do."

The young man eagerly stretched out his hand to grasp the medicine bag, but the owl drew back. "Foolish fellow, suffering from the impatience of youth! If you cannot curb your eagerness and your youthful desires, then even this medicine will be of no help to you."

"I promise to be patient," said the husband.

"Well then," said the owl-man," this is sleep medicine. It will make you fall into a deep sleep and transport you to some other place. When you awake, you will walk toward the Morning Star.

Following the trail to the middle anthill, you will find your spirit-wife there. As the sun rises, so she will rise and smile at you, rise in the flesh, a spirit no more, and so you will live happily.

"But remember to be patient; remember to curb your eagerness. Let not your desire to touch and embrace her get the better of you, for if you touch her before bringing her safely home to the village of your birth, she will be lost to you forever."

Having finished this speech, the old owl-man blew some of the medicine on the young husband's face, who instantly fell into a deep sleep. Then all the strange owl-men put on their owl coats and, lifting the sleeper, flew with him to a place at the beginning of the trail to the middle anthill. There they laid him down underneath some trees.

Then the strange owl-beings flew on to the big lake at the bottom of which the land of the dead was located. The old owl-man's magic sleep medicine, and the feathered prayer sticks which the young man had carved, enabled them to dive down to the bottom of the lake and enter the land of the dead. Once inside, they used the sleep medicine to put to sleep the spirits who are in charge of that strange land beneath the waters. The owl-beings reverently laid their feathered prayer sticks before the altar of that netherworld, took up the beautiful young spirit-wife, and lifted her gently to the surface of the lake. Then, taking her upon their wings, they flew with her to the place where the young husband was sleeping.

When the husband awoke, he saw first the Morning Star, then the middle anthill, and then his wife at his side, still in deep slumber. Then she too awoke and opened her eyes wide, at first not knowing where she was or what had happened to her. When she discovered her lover right by her side, she smiled at him, saying: "Truly, your love for me is strong, stronger than love has ever been, otherwise we would not be here."

They got up and began to walk toward the pueblo of their birth. The young man did not forget the advice the old owl-man had given him, especially the warning to be patient and shun all desire until they had safely arrived at their home. In that way they traveled for four days, and all was well.

On the fourth day they arrived at Thunder Mountain and came to the river that flows by Salt Town. Then the young wife said: "My husband, I am very tired. The journey has been long and the days hot. Let me rest here awhile, let me sleep a while, and then, refreshed, we can walk the last short distance home together." And her husband said: "We will do as you say."

The wife lay down and fell asleep. As her lover was watching over her, gazing at her loveliness, desire so strong that he could not resist it overcame him, and he stretched out his hand and touched her.

She awoke instantly with a start, and, looking at him and at his hand upon her body, began to weep, the tears streaming down her face. At last she said: "You loved me, but you did not love me enough; otherwise you would have waited.

Now I shall die again." And before his eyes her form faded and became transparent, and at the place where she had rested a few moments before, there was nothing. On a branch of a tree above him the old owl-man hooted mournfully: "Shame, shame, shame." Then the young man sank down in despair, burying his face in his hands, and ever after his mind wandered as his eyes stared vacantly.

If the young lover had controlled his desire, if he had not longed to embrace his beautiful wife, if he had not touched her, if he had practiced patience and self-denial for only a short time, then death would have been overcome. There would be no journeying to the land below the lake, and no mourning for others lost

But then, if there were no death, men would crowd each other with more people on this earth than the earth can hold. Then there would be hunger and war, with people fighting over a tiny patch of earth, over an ear of corn, over a scrap of meat. So maybe what happened was for the best.

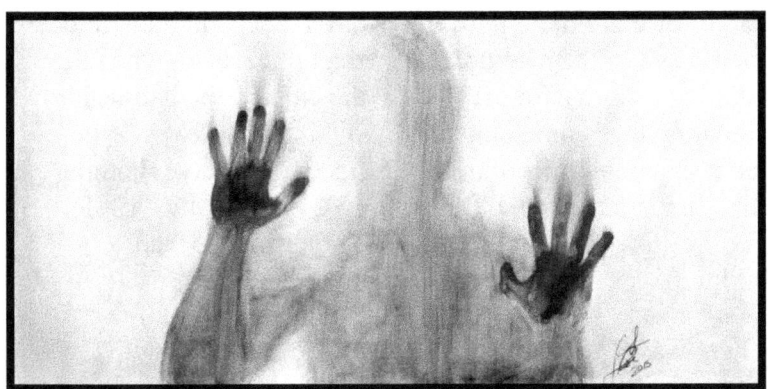

The Nunne'hi And Other Spirit Folk
A Cherokee Legend

The Nûñnë'hï or immortals, the "people who live anywhere," were a race of spirit people who lived in the highlands of the old Cherokee country and had a great many townhouses, especially in the bald mountains.

They had large townhouses in Pilot knob and under the old Nikwasi' mound in North Carolina, and another under Blood mountain, at the head of Nottely River, in Georgia. They were invisible excepting when they wanted to be seen, and then they looked and poke just like other Indians.

They were very fond of music and dancing, and hunters in the mountains would often hear the dance, songs and the drum beating in some invisible townhouse, but when they went toward the sound it would shift about and they would hear it behind them or away in some other direction, so that they could never find the place where the dance was.

They were a friendly people, too, and often brought lost wanderers to their townhouses under the mountains and cared for them there until they were rested and then guided them back to their home . More than once, also, when the Cherokee were hard pressed by the enemy, the Nûñnë'hï warriors have come out, as they did at old Nikwasi', and have saved them from defeat. Some people have thought that they are the same as the Yûñwï Tsunsdi', the "Little People"; but these are fairies, no larger in size than children.

There was a man in Nottely town who had been with the Nûñnë'hï when he was a boy, and he told Wafford all about it. He was a truthful, hard-headed man, and Wafford had heard the story so often from other people that he asked this man to tell it. It was in this way:

When he was about 10 or 12 years old he was playing one day near the river, shooting at a mark with his bow and arrows, until he became tired, and started to build a fish trap in the water. While he was piling up the stones in two long walls a man came and stood on the bank and asked him what he was doing. The boy told him, and the man said, "Well, that's pretty hard work and you ought to rest a while. Come and take a walk up the river."

The boy said, "No"; that he was going home to dinner soon.

"Come right up to my house," said the stranger, and I'll give you a good dinner there and bring you home again in the morning."

So the boy went with him up the river until they came to a house, when they went in, and the man's wife and the other people there were very glad to see him, and gave him a fine dinner, and were very kind to him. While they were eating a man that the boy knew very well came in and spoke to him, so that he felt quite at home.

After dinner he played with the other children and slept there that night, and in the morning, after breakfast, the man got ready to take him home. They went down a path that had a cornfield on one side and a peach orchard fenced in on the other, until they came to another trail, and the man said, "Go along this trail across that ridge and you will come to the river road that will bring you straight to your home, and now I'll go back to the house."

So the man went back to the house and the boy went on along the trail, but when he had gone a little way he looked back, and there was no cornfield or orchard or fence or house; nothing but trees on the mountain side.

He thought it very queer, but somehow he was not frightened, and went on until he came to the river trail in sight of his home. There were a great many people standing about talking, and when they saw him they ran toward him shouting, "Here he is! He is not drowned or killed in the mountains!" They told him they had been hunting him ever since yesterday noon, and asked him where he had been.

"A man took me over to his house just across the ridge, and I had a fine dinner and a good time with the children," said the boy, "I thought Udsi'skalä here"--that was the name of the man he had seen at dinner--"would tell you where I was."

But Udsi'skalä said, "I haven't seen you. I was out all day in my canoe hunting you. It was one of the Nûññë'hï that made himself look like me."

Then his mother said, "You say you had dinner there?"

"Yes, and I had plenty, too," said the boy; but his mother answered, "There is no house there--only trees and rocks--

but we hear a drum sometimes in the big bald above. The people you saw were the Nûñnë'hï."

Once four Nûñnë'hï women came, to a dance at Nottely town, and danced half the night with the young men there, and nobody knew that they were Nûñnë'hï, but thought them visitors from another settlement.

About midnight they left to go home, and some men who had come out from the townhouse to cool off watched to see which way they went. They saw the women go down the trail to the river ford, but just as they came to the water they disappeared, although it was a plain trail, with no place where they could hide.

Then the watchers knew they were Nûñnë'hï women. Several men saw this happen, and one of them was Wafford's father-in-law, who was known for an honest man. At another time a man named Burnt-tobacco was crossing over the ridge from Nottely to Hemptown in Georgia and heard a drum and the songs of dancers in the hills on one side of the trail.

He rode over to see who could be dancing in such a place, but when he reached the spot the drum and the songs were behind him, and he was so frightened that he hurried back to the trail and rode all the way to Hemptown as hard as he could to tell the story. He was a truthful man, and they believed what he said.

There must have been a good many of the Nûñnë'hï living in that neighborhood, because the drumming wits often heard in the high balds almost up to the time of the Removal.

On a small upper branch of Nottely, running nearly due

north from Blood maintain, there was also a hole, like a small well or chimney, in the ground, from which there came up a warm vapor that heated all the air around. People said that this was because the Nûñnë'hï had a townhouse and a fire under the mountain. Sometimes in cold weather hunters would stop there to warm the selves, but they were afraid to stay long. This was more than sixty years ago, but the hole is probably there yet.

Close to the old trading path from South Carolina up to the Cherokee Nation, somewhere near the head of Tugaloo, there was formerly a noted circular depression about the size of a townhouse, and waist deep. Inside it was always clean as though swept by unknown hands. Passing traders would throw logs and rocks into it, but would always, on their return, find them thrown far out from the hole. The Indians said it was a Nunne'hi townhouse, and never liked to go near the place or even to talk about it, until at last some logs thrown in by the traders were allowed to remain there, and then they concluded that the Nunne'hi, annoyed by the persecution of the white men, had abandoned their townhouse forever.

There is another race of spirits, the Yûñwï Tsunsdi', or "Little People," who live in rock eaves on the mountain side. They are little fellows, hardly reaching up to a man's knee, but well shaped and handsome, with long hair falling almost to the ground. They are great wonder workers and are very fond of music, spending half their time drumming and dancing.

They are helpful and kind-hearted, and often when people have been lost in the mountains, especially children who have strayed away from their parents, the Yûñwï Tsunsdi' have found them and taken care of -them and brought them back to their homes. Sometimes their drum is heard in lonely places in the mountains, but it is not safe to follow it, because the Little

People do not like to be disturbed at home, and they throw a spell over the stranger so that he is bewildered and loses his way, and even if he does at last get back to the settlement he is like one dazed ever after.

Sometimes, also, they come near a house at night and the people inside hear them talking, but they must not go out, and in the morning they find the corn gathered or the field cleared as if a whole force of men had been at work. If anyone should go out to watch, he would die. When a hunter finds anything in the woods, such as a knife or a trinket, he must say, "Little People, I want to take this," because it may belong to them, and if he does not ask their permission they will throw stones at him as he goes home.

Once a hunter in winter found tracks in the snow like the tracks of little children. He wondered how they could have come there and followed them until they led him to a cave, which was full of Little People, young and old, men, women, and children. They brought him in and were kind to him, and he was with them some time; but when he left they warned him that he must not tell or he would die.

He went back to the settlement and his friends were all anxious to know where he had been. For a long time he refused to say, until at last he could not hold out any longer, but told the story, and in a few days he died. Only a few years ago two hunters from Raventown, going behind the high fall near the head of Oconaluftee on the East Cherokee reservation, found there a cave with fresh footprints of the Little People all over the floor.

During the smallpox among the East Cherokee just after the

war one sick man wandered off, and his friends searched, but could not find him. After several weeks he came back and said that the Little People had found him and taken him to one of their eaves and tended him until he was cured.

About twenty-five years ago a man named Tsantäwû' was lost in the mountains on the head of Oconaluftee. It was winter time and very cold and his friends thought he must be dead, but after sixteen days he came back and said that the Little People had found him and taken him to their cave, where he had been well treated, and given plenty of everything to eat except bread. This was in large loaves, but when he took them in his hand to eat they seemed to shrink into small cakes so light and crumbly that though he might eat all day he would not be satisfied.

After he was well rested they had brought him a part of the way home until they came to a small creek, about knee deep, when they told him to wade across to reach the main trail on the other side. He waded across and turned to look back, but the Little People were gone and the creek was a deep river. When he reached home his legs were frozen to the knees and he lived only a few days.

Once the Yûñwï Tsunsdi' had been very kind to the people of a certain settlement, helping them at night with their work and taking good care of any lost children, until something happened to offend them and they made up their minds to leave the neighborhood. Those who were watching at the time saw the whole company of Little People come down to the ford of the river and cross over and disappear into the mouth of a large cave on the other side. They were never heard of near the settlement again.

There are other fairies, the Yûñwï Amai'yïnë'hï, or Water-dwellers, who live in the water, and fishermen pray to them for help. Other friendly spirits live in people's houses, although no one can see them, and so long as they are there to protect the house no witch can come near to do mischief.

Tsäwa'sï and Tsäga'sï are the names of two small fairies, who are mischievous enough, but yet often help the hunter who prays to them. Tsäwa'sï, or Tsäwa'sï Usdi'ga (Little Tsäwa'sï), is a tiny fellow, very handsome, with long hair falling down to his feet, who lives in grassy patches on the hillsides and has great power over the game.

To the deer hunter who prays to him he gives skill to slip up on the deer through the long grass without being seen. Tsäga'sï is another of the spirits invoked by the hunter and is very helpful, but when someone trips and falls, we know that it is Tsäga'sï who has caused it. There are several other of these fairies with names, all good-natured, but more or less tricky.

Then there is De'tsätä. De'tsätä was once a boy who ran away to the woods to avoid a scratching and tries to keep himself invisible ever since. He is a handsome little fellow and spends his whole time hunting birds with blowgun and arrow. He has a great many children who are all just like him and have the same name. When a flock of birds flies up suddenly as if frightened it is because De'tsätä is chasing them.

He is mischievous and sometimes hides an arrow from the bird hunter, who may have shot it off into a perfectly clear space, but looks and looks without finding it. Then the hunter says, "De'tsätä, you have my arrow, and if you don't give it up I'll scratch you," and when he looks again he finds it.

There is one spirit that goes about at night with a light. The

Cherokee call it Atsil'dihye'gï, "The Fire-carrier," and they are all afraid of it, because they think it dangerous, although they do not know much about it. They do not even know exactly what it looks like, because they are afraid to stop when they see it. It may be a witch instead of a spirit.

Wafford's mother saw the "Fire-carrier" once when she was a young woman, as she was coming home at night from a trading post in South Carolina. It seemed to be following her from behind, and. she was frightened and whipped up her horse until she got away from it and never saw it again.

The Spirit Defenders Of Nikwasi'
A Cherokee Legend

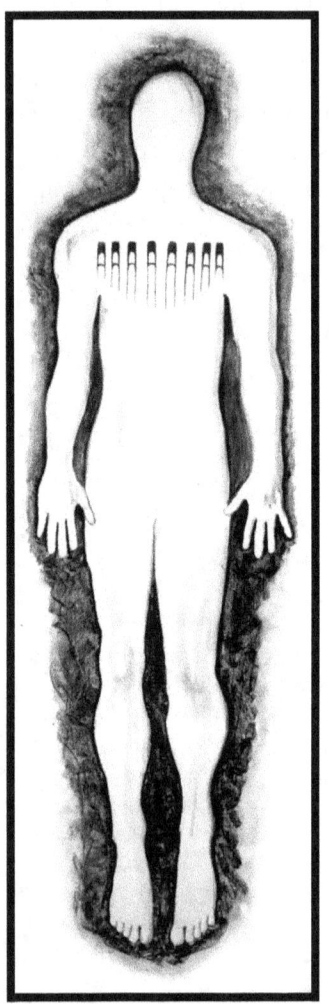

Long ago a powerful unknown tribe invaded the country from the southeast, killing people and destroying settlements wherever they went. No leader could stand against them, and in a little while they had wasted all the lower settlements and advanced into the mountains.

No leader could stand against them, and in a little while they had wasted all the lower settlements and advanced into the mountains.

The warriors of the old town of Nikwasi', on the head of Little Tennessee, gathered their wives and children into the townhouse and kept scouts constantly on the lookout for the presence of danger. One morning just before daybreak the spies saw the enemy approaching and at once gave the alarm.

The Nikwasi' men seized their arms and rushed out to meet the attack, but after a long, hard fight they found themselves overpowered and began to retreat, when suddenly a stranger stood among them and shouted to the chief to call off his men and he himself would drive back the enemy. From the dress and language of the stranger the Nikwasi' people thought him a chief who had come with reinforcements from the Overhill settlements in Tennessee.

They fell back along the trail, and as they came near the townhouse they saw a great company of warriors coming out from the side of the mound as through an open doorway. Then they knew that their friends were the Nûñnë'hï, the Immortals, although no one had ever heard before that they lived under Nikwasi' mound.

The Nûñnë'hï poured out by hundreds, armed and painted for the fight, and the most curious thing about it all was that they became invisible as soon as they were fairly outside of the settlement, so that although the enemy saw the glancing arrow or the rushing tomahawk, and felt the stroke, he could not see who sent it.

Before such invisible foes the invaders soon had to retreat, going first south along the ridge to where joins the main ridge which separates the French Broad from the Tuckasegee, and then turning with it to the northeast. As they retreated they tried to shield themselves behind rocks and trees, but the Nûñnë'hï arrows went around the rocks and killed them from the other side, and they could find no hiding place.

All along the ridge they fell, until when they reached the head of Tuckasegee not more than half a dozen were left alive, and in despair they sat down and cried out for mercy. Ever since then the Cherokee have called the place Dayûlsûñ'yï, "Where they cried."

Then the Nûñnë'hï chief told them they had deserved their punishment for attacking a peaceful tribe, and he spared their lives and told them to go home and take the news to their people. This was the Indian custom, always to spare a few to carry back the news of defeat. They went home toward the north and the Nûñnë'hï went back to the mound.

And they are still there, because, in the last war, when a strong party of Federal troops came to surprise a handful of Confederates posted there they saw so many soldiers guarding the town that they were afraid and went away without making an attack.

The Haunted Whirlpool
Cherokee Legend

At the mouth of Suck creek, on the Tennessee, about 8 miles below Chattanooga, is a series of dangerous whirlpools, known as "The Suck," and noted among the Cherokee as the place where Ûñtsaiyï', the gambler, lived long ago. They call it Ûñ'tiguhï', "Pot-in-the-water," on account of the appearance of the surging, tumbling water, suggesting a boiling pot. They assert that in the old times the whirlpools were intermittent in character, and the canoemen attempting to pass the spot used to hug the bank, keeping constantly on the alert for signs of a coming eruption, and when they saw the water begin to revolve more rapidly would stop and wait until it became quiet again before attempting to proceed.

It happened once that two men, going down the river in a canoe, as they came near this place saw the water circling rapidly ahead of them. They pulled up to the bank to wait until it became smooth again, but the whirlpool seemed to approach with wider and wider circles, until they were drawn into the vortex. They were thrown out of the canoe and carried down under the water, where one man was seized by a great fish and was never seen again. The other was taken round and round down to the very lowest center of the whirlpool, when another circle caught him and bore him outward and upward until he was finally thrown up again to the surface and floated out into the shallow water, whence he made his escape to shore. He told afterwards that when he reached the narrowest circle of the maelstrom the water seemed to open below him and he could look down as through the roof beams of a house, and there on the bottom of the river he had seen a great company of people, who looked up and beckoned to him to join them, but as they put up their hands to seize him the swift current caught him and took him out of their reach.

Deer Hunter and White Corn Woman

Tewa
-Translated from the Tewa by Alfonso Ortiz.

Long ago in the ancient home of the San Juan people, in a village whose ruins can be seen across the river from present-day San Juan, lived two magically gifted young people. The youth was called Deer Hunter because even as a boy, he was the only one who never returned empty-handed from the hunt. The girl, whose name was White Corn Maiden, made the finest pottery, and embroidered clothing with the most beautiful designs, of any woman in the village. These two were the handsomest couple in the village, and it was no surprise to their parents that they always sought one another's company. Seeing that they were favored by the gods, the villagers assumed that they were destined to marry.

And in time they did, and contrary to their elders' expectations, they began to spend even more time with one another. White Corn Maiden began to ignore her pottery making and embroidery, while Deer Hunter gave up hunting, at a time when he could have saved many of his people from hunger. They even began to forget their religious obligations. At the request of the pair's worried parents, the tribal elders called a council. This young couple was ignoring all the traditions by which the tribe had lived and prospered, and the people feared that angry gods might bring famine, Hood, sickness, or some other disaster upon the village.

But Deer Hunter and White Corn Maiden ignored the council's pleas and drew closer together, swearing that nothing would ever part them. A sense of doom pervaded the village, even though it was late spring and all nature had unfolded in new life.

Then suddenly White Corn Maiden became ill, and within three days she died. Deer Hunter's grief had no bounds. He refused to speak or eat, preferring to keep watch beside his wife's body until she was buried early the next day.

For four days after death, every soul wanders in and around its village and seeks forgiveness from those whom it may have wronged in life. It is a time of unease for the living, since the soul may appear in the form of a wind, a disembodied voice, a dream, or even in human shape. To prevent such a visitation, the villagers go to the dead person before burial and utter a soft prayer of forgiveness. And on the fourth day after death, the relatives gather to perform a ceremony releasing the soul into the spirit world, from which it will never return.

But Deer Hunter was unable to accept his wife's death. Knowing that he might see her during the four-day interlude, he began to wander around the edge of the village. Soon he drifted farther out into the fields, and it was here at sundown of the fourth day, even while his relatives were gathering for the ceremony of release, that he spotted a small fire near a clump of bushes.

Deer Hunter drew closer and found his wife, as beautiful as she was in life and dressed in all her finery, combing her long hair with a cactus brush in preparation for the last journey. He fell weeping at her feet, imploring her not to leave but to return with him to the village before the releasing rite was consummated. White Corn Maiden begged her husband to let her go, because she no longer belonged to the world of the living. Her return would anger the spirits, she said, and anyhow, soon she would no longer be beautiful, and Deer Hunter would shun her.

He brushed her pleas aside by pledging his undying love and promising that he would let nothing part them. Eventually she relented, saying that she would hold him to his promise. They entered the village just as their relatives were marching to the shrine with the food offering that would release the soul of White Corn Maiden. They were horrified when they saw her, and again they and the village elders begged Deer Hunter to let her go. He ignored them, and an air of grim expectancy settled over the village.

The couple returned to their home, but before many days had passed, Deer Hunter noticed that his wife was beginning to have an unpleasant odor. Then he saw that her beautiful face had grown ashen and her skin dry. At first he only turned his back on her as they slept. Later he began to sit up on the roof all night, but White Corn Maiden always joined him. In time the villagers became used to the sight of Deer Hunter racing among the houses and through the fields with White Corn Maiden, now not much more than skin and bones, in hot pursuit.

Things continued in this way, until one misty morning a tall and imposing figure appeared in the small dance court at the center of the village. He was dressed in spotless white buckskin robes and carried the biggest bow anyone had ever seen. On his back was slung a great quiver with the two largest arrows anyone had ever seen. He remained standing at the center of the village and called, in a voice that carried into every home, for Deer Hunter and White Corn Maiden. Such was its authority that the couple stepped forward meekly and stood facing him.

The awe-inspiring figure told the couple that he had been sent from the spirit world because they, Deer Hunter and White Corn Maiden, had violated their people's traditions and angered the spirits; that because they had been so selfish, they had brought grief and near-disaster to the village. "Since you insist on being together," he said, "you shall have your wish. You will chase one another forever across the sky, as visible reminders that your people must live according to tradition if they are to survive." With this he set Deer Hunter on one arrow and shot him low into the western sky. Putting White Corn Maiden on the other arrow, he placed her just behind her husband.

That evening the villagers saw two new stars in the west. The first, large and very bright, began to move east across the heavens. The second, a smaller, Bickering star, followed close behind. So it is to this day, according to the Tewa; the brighter one is Deer Hunter, placed there in the prime of his life. The dimmer star is White Corn Maiden, set there after she had died; yet she will forever chase her husband across the heavens.

A Journey to the Skeleton House
Hopi
-Based on a tale collected by Henry Voth in 1905.

Haliksai! In Shongopavi where the people were first living, a curious young man would often sit at the edge of the village looking at the graveyards. He wondered what became of the dead, if they really continued to live somewhere else. He asked his father, who could tell him very little.

His father was the village chief, and he said that he would speak to the other chiefs and to his assistants about it. He asked the village criers whether they knew anything that would help his son. "Yes," they said, "Badger Old Man has the medicine that will answer his questions." So they called Badger Old Man, and when he arrived, they said, "this young man is thinking about the dead-whether they live anywhere. You know about it, and you have medicine that can show him." "Very well," he said, "I'll go and get my medicine."

So he went to his house, looked over his medicines, and finally found the right one. "This is it," he said, and took it to the village chief. "Very well," he said. "Tomorrow put a white kilt on your son and then blacken his chin with toho, with black shale, and tie a small eagle feather to his forehead. These are the very preparations used for the dead." The next morning they dressed the young man in this way, and Badger Old Man spread a white owa on the floor and told the young man to lie on it. He gave the young man some medicine to eat and also placed medicine in his ears and on his heart. Then he wrapped him in a robe, whereupon the young man, after moving a little, "died." "This is the medicine," Badger Old Man said. "If he hears this, he will go far away but he will also come back again. He wanted to see something and find out something, and with this medicine he will do just that."

After the young man had fallen asleep, he saw a path leading westward. It was the road to the skeleton house. This path he followed, and after a while he met a woman sitting by the roadside. "What have you come for?" she asked the young man. "I have come," he replied, "to find out about your life here." "Yes," the other one said, "I didn't follow the straight road; I didn't listen, and I now have to wait here. After a certain number of days I can go on a little, then I can go on again, but it will be a long time before I shall get to skeleton house." She pointed to an enclosure of sticks, which was all the house and protection she had.

From here the path led westward through large cactus and agave plants so full that they sometimes hid the way. He finally arrived at the rim of a steep bluff, where a chief was sitting.

He was a Kwaniita, and had a white line around his right eye and a big horn for a headdress. He also asked the young man why he had come, and the latter told him. "Very well," the chief said.

"Away over there is the house that you are looking for." But a great deal of smoke in the distance hid the house from the young man's view. The chief spread the young man's kilt on the ground, placed the young man on it, then lifted it up. Holding it over the precipice, the chief threw it forward, whereupon the kilt carried the young man slowly down like a giant bird.

When he had arrived on the ground below the bluff, he put on his kilt again and proceeded. In the distance he saw a column of smoke rising. After he had proceeded a distance, he came upon Skeleton Woman and asked her what the smoke was. "Some of those who were wicked while they lived in the village were thrown in there," she said. "The bad chiefs send their people over this road, and then they are destroyed; they no longer exist. You must not go there," she added. "Keep on this road and go straight ahead toward skeleton house."

When at last he arrived at skeleton house, he did not see anyone except a few children playing there. "Oh!" they said, "here a 'skeleton has come," and by the time he went into the village, all the people-or skeletons, rather-living there had heard about him and gathered to stare. 'Who are you?" they asked the young man. "I am the village chief's son. I came from Shongopavi."

So they pointed toward the Bear clan, saying, "Those are the people that you want to see. They are your ancestors." A skeleton took him over to the house where his clan lived and showed him the ladder that led up to the house. The rungs of the ladder were made of sunflower stems, and the first rung broke as soon as he stepped on it, though the skeletons went up and down the ladder with no trouble. "I shall have to stay down here," he said; "bring me food and feed me here." So the skeletons brought him some melon, watermelon, and chukuviki.

When they saw him eat, they laughed at him; they are lighter than air because they never eat the food, but only its odor or soul. And that is the reason why the clouds into which the dead are transformed are not heavy and can float in the air. The food itself the skeletons threw out behind the houses, which is where they got his meal. When he had finished, they asked him what he had come for. He said, "I was wondering whether skeletons lived somewhere. I told my father I wanted to go and find' out, and he dressed me up in this way and Badger Old Man gave me some medicine to make it happen." "So that's what you have come for; well, look at us." Then they added: "It's not light here; it's not as light as where you live. We actually live poorly here. You cannot stay with us here yet; your flesh is still strong and 'salty.' You still eat food; we eat only the odor of the food. But when you go back, you must work there for us. Make nakwakwosis for us at the Soyal ceremony. These we tie around our foreheads, and they represent dropping rain.

We shall work for you here, too. We shall send you rain and crops. You must wrap up in the owa women when they die, and tie the big knotted belt around them, because these owas are not tightly woven. When the skeletons move along on them through the sky as clouds, the thin rain drops through these owas, and the big raindrops fall from the fringes of the big belt. Sometimes you cannot see the clouds distinctly, because they are hidden behind these nakwakwosis, just as our faces are hidden behind them."

Looking around, the young man saw some of the skeletons walking around with huge burdens on their backs. These were mealing stones, which they carried by a thin string over the forehead that had cut deeply into the skin. Others carried bundles of cactus on their backs, and as they had no clothes on, the thorns of the cactus hurt them. He was told that some had to submit to such punishments for a certain length of time, then were relieved of them and could live with the others. At another place in the skeleton house he saw the chiefs who had been good here in this world and had made a good road for other people. They had taken their tiponis, their protective medicine, and set them up there, and when the people here in the villages have their ceremonies and smoke during the ceremonies, this smoke goes down into the other world to the tiponis or mothers and from there rises up in the form of clouds.

After the young man had seen everything and satisfied his curiosity, he set off to his own village. When he arrived at the steep bluff, he again mounted his kilt and a slight breeze lifted him up.

He met the Kwaniita chief, who told him, "Your father and mother are mourning for you now, so you'd better return home." This was the last person he met on his way back.

When he had just about arrived at his house, his body, which was still lying under the covering in the room where he had fallen asleep, began to move, and as they joined once more, it came to life again. They removed the covering, and Badger Old Man wiped his body, washed the paint off his face, and discharmed him. Then he sat up.

They fed him and asked what he had found out. He recounted all of his experiences in detail - the woman with the house of brush, the Kwaniita chief and his Right on a kilt, and all about the skeleton house - the skeletons with heavy burdens of cactus and stones, and even the skeletons' food. "I have seen it all myself now, and I shall remember it. We are living in the light here. They are living in the dark there. No one should desire to go there."

Then he told them about the nakwakwosis and bahos. "If we make prayer offerings for them, they will provide rain

and crops and food for us. Thus we shall assist each other."
"Very well," they all said. "Very well; so that is the way."
And so they returned to their homes wiser than before.

And from that time, the living and the dead began to work together for the benefit of both.

The Elk Spirit Of Lost Lake
Wasco
-Collected by Ella Clark in 1953.

In the days of our grandfathers, a young warrior named Plain Feather lived near Mount Hood. His guardian spirit was a great elk. The great elk taught Plain Feather so well that he knew the best places to look for every kind of game and became the most skillful hunter in his tribe.

Again and again his guardian spirit said to him, "Never kill more than you can use. Kill only for your present need. Then there will be enough for all."

Plain Feather obeyed him. He killed only for food, only what he needed. Other hunters in his tribe teased him for not shooting for fun, for not using all his arrows when he was out on a hunt. But Plain Feather obeyed the great elk.

Smart Crow, one of the old men of the tribe, planned in his bad heart to make the young hunter disobey his guardian spirit. Smart Crow pretended that he was one of the wise men and that he had had a vision. In the vision, he said, the Great Spirit had told him that the coming winter would be long and cold. There would be much snow.

"Kill as many animals as you can," said Smart Crow to the hunters of the tribe. 'We must store meat for the winter."

The hunters, believing him, went to the forest and meadows and killed all the animals they could. Each man tried to be the best hunter in the tribe. At first Plain Feather would not go with them, but Smart Crow kept saying, "The Great Spirit told me that we will have a hard winter. The Great Spirit told me that we must get our meat now."

Plain Feather thought that Smart Crow was telling the truth. So at last he gave in and went hunting along the stream now called Hood River. First he killed deer and bears. Soon he came upon five bands of elk and killed all but one, which he wounded.

Plain Feather did not know that this was his guardian elk, and when the wounded animal hurried away into the forest, Plain Feather followed. Deeper and deeper into the forest and into the mountains he followed the elk tracks. At last he came to a beautiful little lake. There, lying in the water not far from the shore, was the wounded elk. Plain Feather walked into the lake to pull the animal to the shore, but when he touched it, both hunter and elk sank.

The warrior seemed to fall into a deep sleep, and when he awoke, he was on the bottom of the lake. All around him were the spirits of many elk, deer, and bears. All were in the shape of human beings, and all were moaning. He heard a voice say clearly, "Draw him in." And something drew Plain Feather closer to the wounded elk.

"Draw him in," the voice said again. And again Plain Feather was drawn closer to the great elk. At last he lay beside it.

"Why did you disobey me?" asked the elk. "All around you are the spirits of the animals you have killed. I will no longer be your guardian. You have disobeyed me and slain my friends."

Then the voice which had said, "Draw him in," said, "Cast him out." And the spirits cast the hunter out of the water, onto the shore of the lake.

Weary in body and sick at heart, Plain Feather dragged himself to the village where his tribe lived. Slowly he entered his tepee and sank upon the ground.

"I am sick," he said. "I have been in the dwelling place of the lost spirits. And I have lost my guardian spirit, the great elk. He is in the lake of the lost spirits."

Then he lay back and died. Ever after, the Indians called that lake the Lake of the Lost Spirits. Beneath its calm blue waters are the spirits of thousands of the dead. On its clear surface is the face of Mount Hood, which stands as a monument to the lost spirits.

The Fatal Swing
*An Osage Legend
Dorsey, Field Museum:
Anthropological Series,
vii, 26, No. 22*

Once there was a man living by the big water. He was a deer hunter. He would go out and kill wild turkeys and bring them in. Finally, his mother-in-law fell in love with him.

There was a swing by the water, and the old woman and her daughter would swing across it and back. After a while, the old woman partially cut the rope, so that it would break. While the husband was out hunting one day the old woman said to her daughter, "Let us go to the swing, and have some fun."

The old woman got in first, and swung across the water and back. Then the girl got in the swing and she swung across all right, but when she was half-way back, the rope broke in two, and the girl fell into the water and was drowned.

The old woman went home and got supper for her son-in-law. The man came in just at dark, and he missed his wife, and said, "Mother-in-law, where is my wife?" The old woman said, "She has gone to the swing, and has not yet returned." The old woman began to prepare supper for her son-in-law. The man said, "Do not give me any supper."

So he started to cry. The old woman said, "Do not cry; she is dead, and we cannot help it. I will take care of the baby. Your wife got drowned, so she is lost entirely." The man cut off his hair and threw his leggings away and his shirt, and was mourning for his wife. He would go out, and stay a week at a time without eating.

He became very poor. Finally, he said he was going off to stay several days; that he could not help thinking of his wife. He went off and stayed several days, and when he came home he would cry all the time.

One time, when he was out mourning, a rain and thunderstorm came up, and lightning struck all around the tree he was sitting under. He went back home and saw his baby, but stayed out of his sight. Again he went out, and it rained and thundered, and he went up by a big tree and lightning struck a tree near by him.

The Lightning left him a club, and said, "Man, I came here to tell you about your wife for whom you are mourning. You do not know where she is, or how she came to be missing. That old woman drowned her in the big water. The old woman broke the rope and the girl is drowned in the big water. This club you must keep in a safe place. I was sent here to you, and I will help you get your wife back, and you must not be afraid of the big water. Go ahead and try to get her, and the fourth day you will get her all right."

The man went to the big water, and he saw his wife out in the water, and she said, "I cannot get to you. I am tied here with chains. I am going to come up four times." The next time she came out half-way. She said, "Bring me the baby, and I will let her nurse." So the man took the baby to her mother and let her nurse

The woman said, "They are pulling me, and I must go. But the next time you must get me." So she came out the third time up to her knees. The man took the baby to her and let it nurse again. The woman said, "I have got to go back. They are pulling me by the chains. I must go, but the next time will be the last.

I want you to try your best to get me." The man said, "I am going to get you, without doubt." The woman came out the fourth time, and the man hit the chain with the club and it seemed as though lightning struck it, and broke it. He got his wife.

So they went home, and the old woman said, "My daughter, you have got home." But the woman said not a word. Then the man heated an arrow red-hot and put it through the old woman's ears.

So they killed the woman.

The Simpleton's Wisdom

A Sioux Legend
Marie L. McLaughlin, Myths and Legends of the Sioux, 1913

There was a man and his wife who had one daughter. Mother and daughter were deeply attached to one another, and when the latter died the mother was disconsolate.

She cut off her hair, cut gashes in her cheeks and sat before the corpse with her robe drawn over her head, mourning for her dead. She would not let them touch the body to take it to a burying scaffold.

She had a knife in her hand, and if anyone offered to come near the body the mother would wail, "I am weary of life. I do not care to live. I will stab myself with this knife and join my daughter in the land of spirits."

Her husband and relatives tried to get the knife from her, but could not. They feared to use force lest she kill herself. They came together to see what they could do.

"We must get the knife away from her," they said.

At last they called a boy, a kind of simpleton, yet with a good deal of natural shrewdness. He was an orphan and very poor. His moccasins were out at the sole and he was dressed in wei-zi (coarse buffalo skin, smoked).

"Go to the teepee of the mourning mother, " they told the simpleton, "and in some way contrive to make her laugh and forget her grief. Then try to get the knife away from her."

The boy went to the tent and sat down at the door as if waiting to be given something. The corpse lay in the place of honor where the dead girl had slept in life. The body was wrapped in a rich robe and wrapped about with ropes.

Friends had covered it with rich offerings out of respect to the dead.

As the mother sat on the ground with her head covered she did not at first see the boy, who sat silent. But when his reserve had worn away a little he began at first lightly, then more heavily, to drum on the floor with his hands.

After a while he began to sing a comic song. Louder and louder he sang until carried away with his own singing he sprang up and began to dance, at the same time gesturing and making all manner of contortions with his body, still singing the comic song. As he approached the corpse he waved his hands over it in blessing.

The mother put her head out of the blanket and when she saw the poor simpleton with his strange grimaces trying to do honor to the corpse by his solemn waving, and at the same time keeping up his comic song, she burst out laughing. Then she reached over and handed her knife to the simpleton.

"Take this knife," she said. "You have taught me to forget my grief. If while I mourn for the dead I can still be mirthful, there is no reason for me to despair. I no longer care to die. I will live for my husband."

The simpleton left the teepee and brought the knife to the astonished husband and relatives.

"How did you get it? Did you force it away from her, or did you steal it?" they asked.

"She gave it to me. How could I force it from her or steal it when she held it in her hand, blade uppermost? I sang and danced for her and she burst out laughing. Then she gave it to me," he answered.

When the old men of the village heard the orphan's story they were very silent. It was a strange thing for a lad to dance in a teepee where there was mourning. It was stranger that a mother should laugh in a teepee before the corpse of her dead daughter.

The old men gathered at last in a council. They sat a long time without saying anything, for they did not want to decide hastily. The pipe was filled and passed many times. At last an old man spoke.

"We have a hard question. A mother has laughed before the corpse of her daughter, and many think she has done foolishly, but I think the woman did wisely. The lad was simple and of no training, and we cannot expect him to know how to do as well as one with good home and parents to teach him. Besides, he did the best that he knew. He danced to make the mother forget her grief, and he tried to honor the corpse by waving over it his hands."

"The mother did right to laugh, for when one does try to do us good, even if what he does causes us discomfort, we should always remember rather the motive than the deed. And besides, the simpleton's dancing saved the woman's life, for she gave up her knife. In this, too, she did well, for it is always better to live for the living than to die for the dead."

The Ghost Country
Kwakiutl

The ghosts live in four houses, each one deeper than the preceding one. A Koskimo woman was crying on account of her dead father. They buried him and she was crying over the grave for four days. The people called her but she refused to leave. On the fourth day she heard somebody come who called her. "I call you downward, Crying Woman."

Then she jumped up and the ghost said, "Follow me." He went downward and she followed him. They came to a house called Hemlock-Leaves-on-Back. They entered the house and an old woman was sitting near the fire. She said, "Ah, ah, ah, ah. Sit down near the fire." They took poles to take down dry salmon and prepared to roast it. They placed it on a small food mat and broke it up and gave it to Crying Woman.

Just when she was about to take it, a person came in and invited her to another house called Maggots-on-Bark-on-Ground. Then the woman who lived in the first house said, "Ah, ah, ah, ah. Go with her. They are higher in rank than we are." She followed the person who had invited her and entered the next house. She saw an old woman sitting by the fire and seemed to be the same one whom she had seen first. She prepared food in the same way, giving her something to eat.

Just when she was about to eat, another woman came to her and invited her into her house, which was called Place-of-Mouth-Showing-on-Ground. The woman in the second house said, "Go with her. They are higher in rank than we are." When she entered, the same old woman seemed to be sitting by the fire. Again they prepared something for her to eat.

When she was just about to begin, she was called by another person into the fourth house, called Place-of-Never-Return. Again the woman said, "They are higher in rank that we. Go." When she entered she saw her father sitting at the end of the house. And when he saw her he became angry and said, "Why do you come here? This is the place which nobody ever returns. Whoever enters the first three houses may return. But if you come here, you must stay. Do not eat what is offered to you and go back."

Then he called the ghosts to take her back. She was lying under the grave tree like one dead. The ghosts came back singing the following song:

hama yahahaha

She was like one dead when she came back. When her father spoke to her he said, "When we take you back we will sing so that the Koskimo may here our song." They brought her up alive on a board. The people heard the song, but they did not see anyone. Then they took the board into the winter-dance house. This song belongs originally to the Koskimo and was carried from there to the Newettee and to the Nåkwado.

The Legend of the Maid of the Mist

The Legend Of Lelawala

Long ago, the peaceful tribe of the Ongiaras lived beside the Niagara River. For an unknown reason, Indians were dying, and it was believed that the tribe must appease the Thunder God Hinum, who lived with his two sons in a cave behind the Falls.

At first, the Indians sent canoes laden with fruit, flowers and game over the Falls, but the dying continued.

The Indians then began to sacrifice the most beautiful maiden of the tribe, who was selected once a year during a ceremonial feast.

One year, Lelawala, daughter of Chief Eagle Eye was chosen. On the appointed day, Lelawala appeared on the river bank above the Falls, wearing a white doeskin robe with a wreath of woodland flowers in her hair.

She stepped into a white birch bark canoe and plunged over the Falls to her death. Her father, heartbroken, leaped into his canoe and followed her.

Hinum's two sons caught Lelawala in their arms, and each desired her. She promised to accept the one who told her what evil was killing her people.

The younger brother told her of a giant water snake that lay at the bottom of the river. Once a year, the monster snake grew hungry, and at night entered the village and poisoned the water. The snake then devoured the dead.

In spirit, Lelawala told her people to destroy the serpent. Indian braves mortally wounded the snake on his next yearly visit to the village. Returning to his lair on the river, the snake caught his head on one side of the river and his tail on the other, forming a semi-circle and the brink of the Horseshoe Falls. Lelawala returned to the cave of the God Hinum, where she reigns as the Maid of the Mist.

Ghost Stallion
A Yinnuwok Legend

This is a tale the old men tell around the fire, when the stars are blown clean on a windy night, and the coyotes are howling on the Cree Jump. And when, sometimes, over the wind, comes clearly the sound of running horses, their hearers move a little closer to one another and pile more wood on the fire.

This is a story from a long time ago, say the Old Ones. What the man's name was, no one knows now, and so they call him "The Traveler".

Long ago, The Traveler was a wealthy chief. A warrior in his young days, he had taken many scalps, many horses, and many another trophy of value. And he had increased his possessions by hard dealings with that less fortunate, and by gambling with younger men who were no match for his cunning.

His fellow tribesmen did not love him although they admired his bravery, for in times of hardship, when other chiefs shared freely whatever they had, he drove hard bargains and generally prospered from the ills of others. His wives he had abused till their parents took them away; his children hated him, and he had no love for them.

There was only one thing he cared for: his horses. They were fine horses, beautiful horses, for he kept only the best; and when a young warrior returned from a raid with a particularly good horse, The Traveler never rested until (whether by fair means or not) he had it in his possession. At night, when the dance drum was brought out, and the other Indians gathered round it, The Traveler went alone to the place where his horses were picketed, to gloat over his treasures. He loved them. But he loved only the ones that were young, and handsome, and healthy a horse that was old, or sick, or injured, received only abuse.

One morning, when he went to the little valley in which his horses were kept, he found in the herd an ugly white stallion. He was old, with crooked legs, and a matted coat, thin, and tired looking.

The Traveler flew into a rage. He took his rawhide rope, and caught the poor old horse. Then, with a club, he beat him unmercifully. When the animal fell to the ground, stunned, The Traveler broke his legs with the club, and left him to die. He returned to his lodge, feeling not the slightest remorse for his cruelty.

Later, deciding he might as well have the hide of the old horse, he returned to the place where he had left him. But, to his surprise, the white stallion was gone. That night, as The Traveler slept, he had a dream. The white stallion appeared to him, and slowly turned into a beautiful horse, shining white, with long mane and tail - a horse more lovely than any The Traveler had ever seen.

Then the Stallion spoke: "If you had treated me kindly," the stallion said, "I would have brought you more horses. You were cruel to me, so I shall take away the horses you have!"

When The Traveler awoke, he found his horses were gone. All that day, he walked and searched, but when at nightfall he fell asleep exhausted, he had found no trace of them. In his dreams, the White Stallion came again, and said, "Do you wish to find your horses? They are north, by a lake. You will sleep twice, before you come to it."

As soon as he awakened in the morning, The Traveler hastened northward. Two days' journey, and when he came to the lake there were no horses. That night, the Ghost Stallion came again. "Do you wish to find your horses?" he said. "They are east, in some hills. There will be two sleeps before you came to the place.'

When the sun had gone down on the third day, The Traveler had searched the hills, but had found no horses. And so it went night after night the Stallion came to The Traveler, directing him to some distant spot, but he never found his horses. He grew thin, and his feet were sore. Sometimes he got a horse from some friendly camp; sometimes he stole one, in the night. But always, before morning, would come a loud drumming of hoofs, the Ghost Stallion and his band would gallop by, and the horse of The Traveler would break its picket, and go with them.

And never again did he have a horse; never again did he see his own lodge. And he wanders, even to this day, the old men say, still searching for his lost horses.

Sometimes, they say, on a windy autumn night when the stars shine very clearly, and over on the Cree Jump the coyote's howl, above the wind you may hear a rush of running horses, and the stumbling footsteps of an old man. And, if you are very unlucky, you may see the Stallion and his band, and The Traveler, still pursuing them, still trying to get back his beautiful horses.

Song of the Ghost Dance
A Paiute Legend
Katharine Berry Judson, Myths and Legends of California and the Old Southwest, 1912

The snow lies there - ro-rani!
The snow lies there - ro-rani!
The snow lies there - ro-rani!
The snow lies there - ro-rani!
The Milky Way lies there.
The Milky Way lies there.

"This is one of the favorite songs of the Paiute Ghost dance. . . . It must be remembered that the dance is held in the open air at night, with the stars shining down on the wide-extending plain walled in by the giant Sierras, fringed at the base with dark pines, and with their peaks white with eternal snows.

Under such circumstances this song of the snow lying white upon the mountains, and the Milky Way stretching across the clear sky, brings up to the Paiute the same patriotic home love that comes from lyrics of singing birds and leafy trees and still waters to the people of more favored regions. . . .

The Milky Way is the road of the dead to the spirit world."

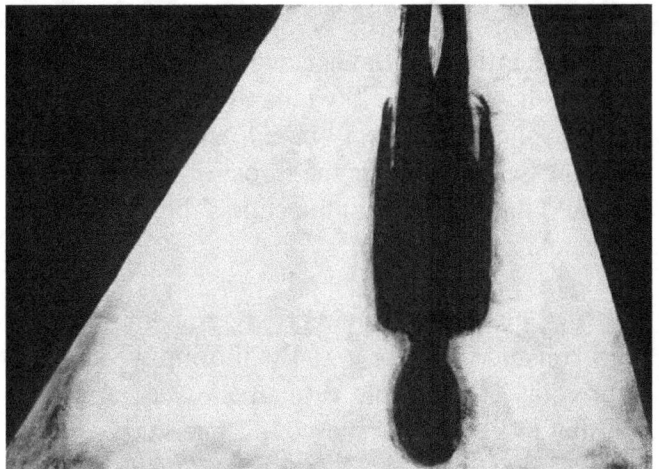

The Deserted Children
A Gros Ventre Legend

There was a camp. All the children went off to play. They went to some distance. Then one man said, "Let us abandon the children. Lift the ends of your tent-poles and travois when you go, so that there will be no trail."

Then the people went off. After a time the oldest girl amongst the children sent the others back to the camp to get something to eat. The children found the camp gone, the fires out, and only ashes about. They cried, and wandered about at random. The oldest girl said, "Let us go toward the river."

They found a trail leading across the river, and forded the river there. Then one of the girls found a tent-pole. As they went along, she cried, "My mother, here is your tent-pole." "Bring my tent-pole here!" shouted an old woman loudly from out of the timber. The children went towards her.

They found that she was an old woman who lived alone. They entered her tent. At night they were tired. The old woman told them all to sleep with their heads toward the fire. Only one little girl who had a small brother pretended to sleep, but did not. The old woman watched if all were asleep. Then she put her foot in the fire. It became red hot. Then she pressed it down on the throat of one of the children, and burned through the child's throat. Then she killed the next one and the next one.

The little girl jumped up, saying, "My grandmother, let me live with you and work for you. I will bring wood and water for you." Then the old woman allowed her and her little brother to live. "Take these out," she said.

Then the little girl, carrying her brother on her back, dragged out the bodies of the other children. Then the old woman sent her to get wood. The little girl brought back a load of cottonwood. When she brought it, the old woman said, "That is not the kind of wood I use. Throw it out. Bring another load." The little girl went out and got willow-wood. She came back, and said, "My grandmother, I have a load of wood." "Throw it in," said the old woman.

The little girl threw the wood into the tent. The old woman said, "That is not the kind of wood I use. Throw it outside. Now go get wood for me." Then the little girl brought birch-wood, then cherry, then sagebrush; but the old woman always said, "That is not the kind of wood I use," and sent her out again. The little girl went.

She cried and cried. Then a bird came to her and told her, " Bring her ghost- ropes for she is a ghost." Then the little girl brought some of these plants, which grow on willows. The old woman said, "Throw in the wood which you have brought." The little girl threw it in. Then the old woman was glad. "You are my good grand-daughter," she said.

Then the old woman sent the little girl to get water. The little girl brought her river-water, then rain-water, then spring-water; but the old woman always told her, "That is not the kind of water I use. Spill it!" Then the bird told the little girl, "Bring her foul, stagnant water, which is muddy and full of worms. That is the only kind she drinks." The little girl got the water, and when she brought it the old woman was glad.

Then the little boy said that he needed to go out doors. "Well, then, go out with your brother, but let half of your robe remain inside of the tent while you hold him." Then the girl took her little brother out, leaving half of her robe inside the tent. When she was outside, she stuck an awl in the ground. She hung her robe on this, and, taking her little brother, fled.

The old woman called, "Hurry!" Then the awl answered, "My grandmother, my little brother is not yet ready." Again the old woman said, "Now hurry!" Then the awl answered again, "My little brother is not ready." Then the old woman said, "Come in now; else I will go outside and kill you." She started to go out, and stepped on the awl.

The little girl and her brother fled, and came to a large river An animal with two horns lay there. It said, "Louse me." The little boy loused it. Its lice were frogs. "Catch four, and crack them with your teeth," said the Water-monster. The boy had on a necklace of plum-seeds. Four times the girl cracked a seed. She made the monster think that her brother had cracked one of its lice. Then the Water-monster said, "Go between my horns, and do not open your eyes until we have crossed." Then he went under the surface of the water. He came up on the other side. The children got off and went on.

The old woman was pursuing the children, saying, "I will kill you. You cannot escape me by going to the sky or by entering the ground." She came to the river. The monster had returned, and was lying at the edge of the water. "Louse me," it said. The old woman found a frog. "These dirty lice! I will not put them into my mouth!" she said, and threw it into the river. She found three more, and threw them away. Then she went on the Water-monster. He went under the surface of the water, remained there, drowned her, and ate her. The children went on.

At last they came to the camp of the people who had deserted them. They came to their parents' tent. "My mother, here is your little son," the girl said. "I did not know that I had a son," their mother said. They went to their father, their uncle, and their grandfather. They all said, "I did not know I had a son," "I did not know I had a nephew," "I did not know I had a grandson." Then a man said, "Let us tie them face to face, and hang them in a tree and leave them."

Then they tied them together, hung them in a tree, put out all the fires, and left them. A small dog with sores all over his body, his mouth, and his eyes, pretended to be sick and unable to move, and lay on the ground. He kept a little fire between his legs, and had hidden a knife. The people left the dog lying. When they had all gone off, the dog went to the children, climbed the tree, cut the ropes, and freed them. The little boy cried and cried. He felt bad about what the people had done.

Then many buffalo came near them. "Look at the buffalo, my brother," said the girl. The boy looked at the buffalo, and they fell dead. The girl wondered how they might cut them up. "Look at the meat, my younger brother," she said. The boy looked at the dead buffalo, and the meat was all cut up. Then she told him to look at the meat, and when he looked at it, the meat was dried. Then they had much to eat, and the dog became well again.

The girl sat down on the pile of buffalo-skins, and they were all dressed. She folded them together, sat on them, and there was a tent. Then she went out with the dog and looked for sticks. She brought dead branches, broken tent-poles, and rotten wood. "Look at the tent-poles," she said to her brother. When he looked, there were large straight tent-poles, smooth and good. Then the girl tied three together at the top, and stood them up, and told her brother to look at the tent.

He looked, and a large fine tent stood there. Then she told him to go inside and look about him. He went in and looked. Then the tent was filled with property, and there were beds for them, and a bed also for the dog. The dog was an old man. Then the girl said, "Look at the antelopes running, my brother." The boy looked, and the antelopes fell dead. He looked at them again, and the meat was cut up and the skins taken off.

Then the girl made fine dresses of the skins for her brother and herself and the dog. Then she called as if she were calling for dogs, and four bears came loping to her. "You watch that pile of meat, and you this one," she said to each one of the bears. The bears went to the meat and watched it. Then the boy looked at the woods and there was a corral full of fine painted horses. Then the children lived at this place, the same place where they had been tied and abandoned. They had very much food and much property.

Then a man came and saw their tent and the abundance they had, and went back and told the people. Then the people were told, "Break camp and move to the children for we are without food." Then they broke camp and traveled, and came to the children.

The women went to take meat, but the bears drove them away. The girl and her brother would not come out of the tent. Not even the dog would come out. Then the girl said, "I will go out and bring a wife for you, my brother, and for the dog, and a husband for myself."

Then she went out, and went to the camp and selected two pretty girls and one good-looking young man, and told them to come with her. She took them into the tent, and the girls sat down by the boy and the old man, and the man by her. Then they gave them fine clothing, and married them. Then the sister told her brother, "Go outside and look at the camp." The boy went out and looked at the people, and they all fell dead.

How the Worm Pipe Came to the Blackfoot

As told to anthropologist George Bird Grinnell, 1900

Family affection is one of the most striking characteristics of the Indian, and permeates all his legend and folklore. It is the motive which induces many a hero to start off on his travels, striving to accomplish some great thing. Stories having this motive are Comanche Chief and the Ghost Wife in Pawnee, and Scarface and the Origin of the Worm Pipe in Blackfoot literature. An abstract of this last tale will give an idea of its character, and incidentally show its resemblance to one of the most familiar classical myths. -- GBG

There was once a man who was very fond of his wife. After they had been married for some time they had a little boy. After that the woman fell sick and did not get well. The young man loved his wife so dearly that he did not wish to take a second wife. She grew worse and worse. Doctoring did not seem to do her any good, and at last she died.

The man used to take his baby on his back and travel out from the camp, walking over the hills crying. He kept away from the village. After some time he said to his child, "My little boy, you will have to go and live with your grandmother. I am going to try to find your mother and bring her back."

He took the baby to his mother's lodge and asked her to take care of him, and left it with her. Then he started off to look for his wife, not knowing where he was going nor what he was going to do.

He traveled toward the land of the dead; and after long journeyings, by the assistance of helpers who had spiritual power, he reached it. The old woman who helped him to get there told him how hard it was to penetrate to the ghosts' country, and made him understand that the shadows would try to scare him by making fearful noises and showing him strange and terrible things. At last he reached the ghosts' camp, and as he passed through it the ghosts tried to scare him by all kinds of fearful sights and sounds, but he kept up a brave heart.

He reached a lodge, and the man who owned it came out and asked him where he was going. He said, "I am looking for my dead wife. I mourn for her so much that I cannot rest. My littleboy, too, keeps crying for his mother. They have offered to give me other wives, but I do not want them. I want only the one for whom I am searching."

The ghost said to him: "It is a fearful thing that you have come here. It is very likely that you will never get away. There never was a person here before." But the ghost asked him to come into the lodge, and he entered.

Then this chief ghost said to him: "You shall stay here for four nights, and you shall see your wife; but you must be very careful or you will never go back. You will die right here."

Then the chief went outside and called for a feast, inviting this man's father-in-law and other relations who were in the camp, saying, "Your son-in-law invites you to a feast," as if to say that their son-in-law was dead, and had become a ghost, and had arrived at the ghosts' camp. Now when these invited people, the relations and some of the principal men of the camp, had reached the lodge, they did not like to go in. They called out, "There is a person here!"

It seemed that there was something about him that they could not bear the smell of. The ghost chief burned sweet pine in the fire, which took away this smell, and the people came in and sat down.

Then the host said to them: "Now pity this son-in-law of yours. He is seeking his wife. Neither the great distance nor the fearful sights that he has seen here have weakened his heart. You can see for yourselves he is tender-hearted. He not only mourns for his wife, but mourns also because his little boy is now alone, with no mother; so pity him and give him back his wife."

After consultation the ghosts determined that they would give him back his wife, who should become alive again. They also gave him a sacred pipe. And at last, after many difficulties, the man and his wife reached their home.

Tale of Coyote and the Origin of Death

Dorsey, George A. Traditions of the Caddo. Washington: Carnegie Institution. 1905.

In the beginning of this world there was no such thing as death. Every one continued to live until there were so many people that there was not room for any more on the earth. The chiefs held a council to determine what to do. One man arose and said that he thought it would be a good plan to have the people die and be gone for a little while, and then to return. As soon as he sat down Coyote jumped up and said that he thought that people ought to die forever, for this little world was not large enough to hold all of the people, and if the people who died came back to life there would not be food enough for all. All of the other men objected, saying that they did not want their friends and relatives to die and be gone forever, for then people would grieve and worry and there would not be any happiness in the world.

All except Coyote decided to have the people die and be gone for a little while, and then to come back to life.

The medicine-men built a large grass house facing the east, and when they had completed it they called all of the men of the tribe together and told them that they had decided to have the people who died come to the medicine-house and there be restored to life. The chief medicine-man said that he would put a large white and black eagle feather on top of the grass house, and that when the feather became bloody and fell over, the people would know that some one had died. Then all of the medicine-men were to come to the grass house and sing. They would sing a song that would call the spirit of the dead to the grass house, and when the spirit came they would cause it to assume the form that it had while living, and then they would restore it to life again. All of the people were glad when the medicinemen announced these rules about death, for they were anxious for the dead to be restored to life and come again to live with them.

After a time they saw the eagle feather turn bloody and fall, and so they knew that some one had died. The medicine-men assembled in the grass house and sang, as they had promised that they would, for the spirit of the dead to come to them. In about ten days a whirlwind blew from the west, circled about the grass house, and finally, entered through the entrance in the east. From the whirlwind appeared a handsome young man who had been murdered by another tribe. All of the people saw him and rejoiced except Coyote, who was displeased because his rules about dead were not carried out. In a short time the feather became bloody and fell again. Coyote saw it and at once went to the grass house. He took his seat near the door, and there sat with the singers for many days, and when at last he heard the whirlwind coming he slipped near the door, and as the whirlwind circled about the house and was about to enter, he closed the door. The spirit in the whirlwind, finding the door closed, whirled on by. Death forever was then introduced, and people from that time on grieved about the dead and were unhappy. Now whenever any one meets a whirlwind or hears the wind whistle he says: "There is some one wandering about." Ever since Coyote closed the door the spirits of the dead have wandered over the earth, trying to find some place to go, until at last they find the road to spirit land.

Coyote jumped up and ran away and never came back, for when he saw what he had done he was afraid. Ever after that he ran from one place to another, always looking back over first one shoulder and then over the other, to see if any one was pursuing him, and ever since then he has been starving, for no one will give him anything to eat.

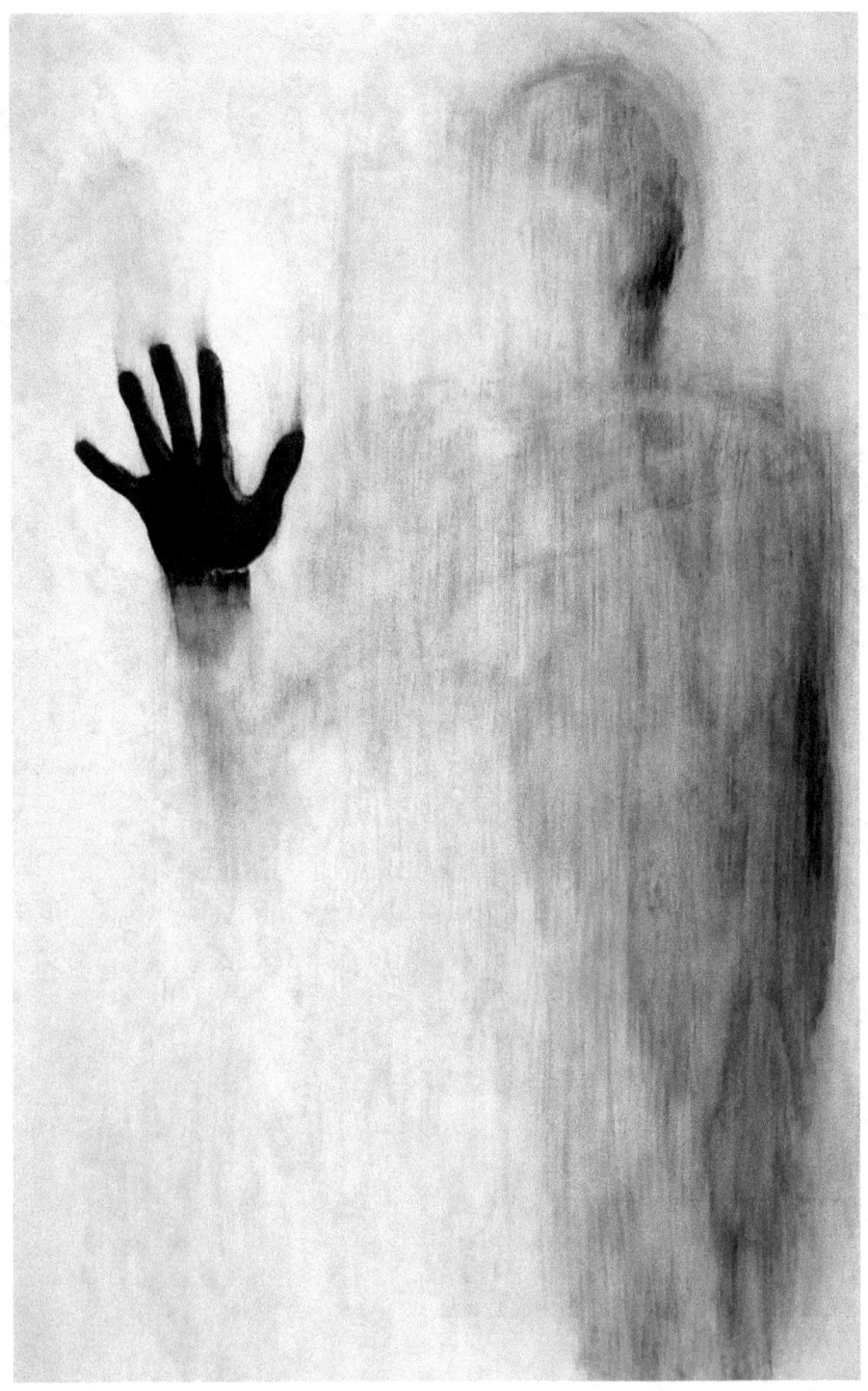